KU-380-881

EAT
GOOD
FOOD

Seriously delicious food that's actually good for you

EAT
GOOD
FOOD

Seriously delicious food that's actually good for you

Contents

EAT WELL
TO LIVE WELL

For as long as I can remember my passion has been to inspire women towards Active Living.

It's my personal life philosophy and undoubtedly the secret to my positive outlook, abundant energy, and overall good health and happiness.

What surprises most people about Active Living is that it makes being fit and healthy incredibly easy. There are no strict guidelines or hard-and-fast rules, just the simple decision to be fitter, healthier and more positive every day.

It's as simple as waking up each morning and setting your intention to:

Move your body with regular exercise;

Nourish your body with foods that are good for you;

And believe in yourself enough to know that you can achieve good health when you decide to make it a priority.

I can't imagine a day without practising Move Nourish Believe because I know firsthand how it can absolutely transform your life. And I'm living proof that every one of you can change for the better if you simply make the decision to put your health and wellbeing first.

It goes without saying that it would be difficult to live an amazing life without good health, and when it comes to being healthy (and Active Living), I believe that food is one of the easiest and most efficient ways to get started – because I know that when you get your food right, everything else just falls into place.

When you start to eat well you'll find you have more energy to workout, you'll think more clearly, have a more positive mindset, feel happier, and have a mind and body that is capable enough to do all the things you want to achieve. If you want to reach your full potential in life, then you need to acknowledge that what you choose to eat really does affect everything else that you do.

I wrote this book to show you that being healthy doesn't have to be about calorie counting, deprivation or boring food. And that all you need to do to feel vibrant and full of energy is EAT GOOD FOOD!

The recipes in this book are some of my favourites, and they'll show you that healthy food can be seriously delicious, and that eating your way to good health can be so enjoyable that you'll want to EAT GOOD FOOD for the rest of your life.

So let's get started!

Lorna Jane Clarkson

YOU ARE WHAT YOU EAT

If you honestly want to look after yourself, both physically and mentally, you need to take care of the way you feed yourself first.

I believe the connection between what we eat and the way we look, think and feel is incredibly powerful. Because not only does food play a vital role in supporting our overall health, but it also affects our mental and emotional wellbeing, and is subsequently a huge contributing factor to what we achieve (or don't achieve) in our lives.

We need to stop and consider how we think about food, and we need to start nourishing our bodies with what humans are actually designed to eat – that is, unprocessed, nutritious, natural, in-season, whole and delicious foods. We need to stay clear of overly-processed foods and instead focus on eating whole ingredients, such as fruits, vegetables, nuts, seeds, legumes, eggs, wholegrains, good-quality protein and healthy fats. And let's not forget the number one essential ingredient for good health – water!

I choose water over any other beverage and drink at least eight glasses a day. And I do this because water really is the elixir of life – it boosts your metabolism, reduces food cravings, detoxes your body and keeps your energy levels high.

Water is also, without doubt, the oldest and cheapest anti-aging potion on the planet, and our bodies need it in abundance for every one of our cells, tissues and organs to function at their best. The more fresh and clean water we consume, the more efficiently every process in our bodies will perform, and as a result we'll look and feel better – and who doesn't want that!

7

SIMPLE WAYS
TO STAY HYDRATED

1. DRINK AS SOON AS YOU WAKE UP (I HAVE A BOTTLE BY THE SIDE OF MY BED AND DRINK 600ML AS SOON AS I OPEN MY EYES).

----

2. EAT FRUIT AND VEGETABLES WITH A HIGH WATER CONTENT. (CUCUMBERS, CELERY, WATERMELON, STRAWBERRIES).

----

3. KEEP IT AT ROOM TEMPERATURE TO MAXIMISE HYDRATION.

----

4. MAKE YOUR WATER DELICIOUS BY ADDING FRUIT (TRY LEMON AND LIME OR STRAWBERRY AND MINT).

----

5. ALWAYS HAVE WATER HANDY (CARRY A REFILLABLE WATER BOTTLE WITH YOU WHEREVER YOU GO).

----

6. DON'T WAIT UNTIL YOU'RE THIRSTY – TRAIN YOURSELF TO SIP REGULARLY.

----

7. TRY NOT TO DRINK WATER WITH YOUR MEALS AS IT CAN INTERFERE WITH DIGESTION.

START PAYING ATTENTION

Another thing I recommend when changing the way you think about food is to eat more mindfully. Eating should be a pleasure and not something done absentmindedly, so try to be present when you're eating and take the time to enjoy the food (and people) in front of you.

START BY

1. SITTING AT A TABLE – AND BEING CONSCIOUS OF YOUR BODY; SIT UP STRAIGHT SO YOUR FOOD CAN MOVE THROUGH YOUR BODY MORE EASILY.

2. BAN ALL DISTRACTIONS – THE TV, COMPUTER, YOUR PHONE, BOOKS OR MAGAZINES – SO THAT YOU CAN THINK ABOUT, AND ENJOY, WHAT YOU ARE EATING INSTEAD.

3. EAT SLOWLY: START BY CHEWING EACH MOUTHFUL 10 TIMES (AIMING FOR 20 OVER TIME) TO EFFECTIVELY PREPARE YOUR FOOD FOR DIGESTION, REDUCE THE ACIDITY IN YOUR FOOD AND INCREASE NUTRITIONAL UPTAKE.

4. TUNE IN TO YOUR BODY: PAY ATTENTION TO WHEN YOU START TO FEEL FULL OR IF PARTICULAR FOODS MAKES YOU FEEL BLOATED OR ANXIOUS (SO YOU CAN CHOOSE TO REDUCE OR ELIMINATE THESE FOODS IN THE FUTURE).

When you start to eat more mindfully, you'll be amazed at how easily you can retrain your brain to make positive choices about the food you eat, how much you eat and what your body actually needs.

KNOW WHEN TO EAT

My philosophy with food is to eat according to what you feel your body needs for the day. I think it's important not to be greedy, but not to deprive yourself either. Listen to your body, think about what you need to achieve your goals, and then give yourself the nourishment you require to be at your best.

I believe that loading up your body with food three times a day is a cultural habit, not a biological one, and I recommend you eat smaller meals more often to give yourself a steady stream of nutrients, keep your blood sugar consistent, and give yourself enough energy to feel good throughout your day.

Eating smaller meals is also less taxing on your digestive system, and the good news is that it actually reduces your risk of heart disease.

A GOOD PLACE TO START...

AS SOON AS YOU WAKE UP, DRINK 600ML OF WATER (WARM OR COLD AND WITH A LITTLE LEMON, IF YOU LIKE) TO BOOST HYDRATION AND GET YOUR BOWELS MOVING!

EAT A WELL-BALANCED BREAKFAST – ANY OF THE ONES IN THIS BOOK ARE GOOD. PERSONALLY, I ALWAYS THINK ABOUT WHAT I HAVE TO DO FOR THE DAY AHEAD AND CHOOSE MY BREAKFAST ACCORDINGLY. IF MY MORNING IS SUPER-BUSY, I'LL CHOOSE SOMETHING A LITTLE HIGHER IN CARBS; IF MY WORKOUT WAS STRENGTH-TRAINING, I'LL CHOOSE SOMETHING HIGHER IN PROTEIN; AND IF I'M IN A RUSH, I MAKE SURE I HAVE A SUPERCHARGED TONIC BEFORE I HEAD OUT THE DOOR, AND TAKE A SMOOTHIE WITH ME SO I CAN SIP IT THROUGHOUT THE MORNING.

ALWAYS HAVE HEALTHY SNACKS ON HAND, BUT MAKE SURE YOU'RE HUNGRY WHEN YOU EAT AGAIN. WAITING THREE HOURS IS A GOOD STARTING POINT, BUT IF YOU FIND YOURSELF GETTING SHAKY, IRRITABLE OR TIRED, YOU MAY NEED TO INCORPORATE SMALLER SNACKS EVERY COUPLE OF HOURS.

FOR LUNCH, EAT PLENTY OF GREENS AND COLOURFUL VEGETABLES, GOOD-QUALITY PROTEIN, SOME UNPROCESSED CARBS AND HEALTHY FATS.

FOR DINNER, GO FOR GREENS AGAIN, MORE VEGIES, A LITTLE LESS UNPROCESSED CARBS, MORE PROTEIN AND HEALTHY FATS. I ALWAYS AIM TO FINISH EATING A FEW HOURS BEFORE SLEEP, GIVING MY BODY TIME TO DIGEST MY FOOD AND TO ENSURE THAT MY GUT IS RELAXED WHEN I TURN OFF THE LIGHTS AND GO TO SLEEP.

KNOW HOW MUCH TO EAT

The most important thing to consider when deciding how much to eat is not to deprive yourself or count calories. Portion size can often get a little confusing and it's important to know that there's not a one-size-fits-all solution. But there are a few things that you can do to make it easier to stay on track:

1. Fill your plate predominantly with vegetables, then smaller portions of protein, starchy carbohydrates and healthy fats. The general rule of thumb is that half of your meal should be vegetables, a quarter protein, and the last quarter a combination of starch together with a little healthy fat.

2. Use smaller plates and bowls.

3. Resist the temptation to over-fill your plate or go back for seconds by stashing any leftovers in a container for lunch or dinner the next day.

4. Choose smaller spoons and bowls when eating dessert.

THE IMPORTANCE OF PLANNING

Now, I'm not an advocate for counting calories or following strict eating plans, but planning your meals and doing a little meal prep on the weekend (ahead of a busy week) is a great way to stay on track with eating healthily.

I love to meal prep and most Sunday afternoons you'll find me in the kitchen getting my food ready for the week ahead. And although I try to buy most of my produce as fresh as possible, I also like to make sure I have plenty of hunger-busting, meal-building ingredients and pre-made meals bursting out of my pantry and fridge for whenever I might need them.

SO WHAT'S IN MY FRIDGE, FREEZER AND PANTRY?

FRIDGE

AN ABUNDANCE OF FRUIT
  & VEGETABLES
NUT MYLKS
YOGHURT
CHEESES
FREE-RANGE EGGS
PROTEIN (MEAT, FISH, TOFU)
FRESH HERBS & SPICES
PURE MAPLE SYRUP
MANUKA HONEY
BEE POLLEN
NUT BUTTERS
MEDJOOL DATES
FERMENTED FOODS
DRESSINGS
APPLE CIDER VINEGAR
MAYONNAISE
MUSTARDS
KOMBUCHA
COCONUT WATER
FRESH YOUNG COCONUTS

FREEZER

HOMEMADE MEALS
SMOOTHIE PACKS
FROZEN BANANAS, BERRIES
  & OTHER FRUITS
FROZEN PEAS, BROAD BEANS
  & EDAMAME
HOMEMADE COOKIES
BLISS BALLS
WHOLEMEAL WRAPS

PANTRY

COLD-PRESSED EXTRA-VIRGIN
  OLIVE OIL
COLD-PRESSED EXTRA-VIRGIN
  COCONUT OIL
ESSENTIAL OILS
NUTS
SEEDS
CHIA SEEDS
CACAO POWDER & NIBS
PROTEIN POWDER
HOMEMADE GRANOLA
OATS
CANNED TOMATOES
CANNED BEANS
CANNED COCONUT MILK
BROWN RICE FLOUR
SPELT FLOUR
BESAN FLOUR
BROWN RICE
BASMATI RICE
RED RICE
LENTILS
BARLEY
QUINOA
TAHINI
SPICES
STOCK
PINK SALT
HERBAL TEAS

TIPS

It's important that you don't sabotage yourself – if you want to eat healthily, then you need to get ready. Think about it – if there's no unhealthy food in your house, then you won't be able to eat it. But if there's junk food around, you'll be sure to grab it when your best intentions are waivering – and believe me, it happens to the best of us!

EATING PLAN TO GET YOU STARTED

A balanced meal plan designed to help you eliminate processed foods
from your diet and get you started on the road to healthy eating.

	SUNDAY	MONDAY	TUESDAY	
WAKE UP	CALM ME TONIC (P24)	METABOLISM BOOSTING TONIC (P28)	METABOLISM BOOSTING TONIC (P28)	
BREAKFAST	SUPERFOOD BREKKIE BOWL (P76)	BLUEBERRY CHIA BIRCHER WITH CINNAMON GRANOLA (P42)	BAKED EGGS WITH KIMCHI (P66)	
LUNCH	PRAWN TACOS WITH CAULIFLOWER TORTILLAS (P113)	PUMPKIN & CAULIFLOWER SOUP WITH TAHINI CREAM (P87)	SALMON POKE BOWL (P105)	
DINNER	LAMB & BUCKWHEAT KOFTAS (P198)	PICK-YOUR-PROTEIN CURRY (P181)	SOCCA PIZZA WITH ZUCCHINI, TOMATO & GOAT'S CHEESE (P164)	
SNACKS	COCONUT, PECAN & APRICOT BAR (P138) INCREDIBLE SEED BREAD (P149)	CARROT & TURMERIC HUMMUS WITH SUMAC CHIPS (P127) INCREDIBLE SEED BREAD (P149)	COCONUT, PECAN & APRICOT BAR (P138) TOASTED NORI CHIPS (P124)	

WEDNESDAY	THURSDAY	FRIDAY	SATURDAY
CALM ME TONIC (P24)	GLOWING SKIN TONIC (P24)	CALM ME TONIC (P24)	GLOWING SKIN TONIC (P24)
BLUEBERRY CHIA BIRCHER WITH CINNAMON GRANOLA (P42)	OMELETTE (P65)	COCONUT & APRICOT NO-GRAIN MUESLI (P55)	MUSHROOM & LABNE FRENCH TOAST (P69)
EDAMAME FALAFEL WRAPS (P110)	SOBA NOODLE & TUNA SALAD (P95)	PUMPKIN & CAULIFLOWER SOUP WITH TAHINI CREAM (P87)	WASABI CHICKEN WITH CUCUMBER & ASPARAGUS SALAD (P102)
TOM YUM PRAWN BROCCOLI 'FRIED RICE' (P173)	CHICKEN SKEWERS WITH KIMCHI SLAW (P159)	POLENTA-CRUSTED FISH WITH PARSNIP MASH & SALSA (P174)	AYURVEDIC BEEF CURRY WITH CAULIFLOWER RICE & RAITA (P187)
CARROT & TURMERIC HUMMUS WITH SUMAC CHIPS (P127) INCREDIBLE SEED BREAD (P149)	COCONUT, PECAN & APRICOT BAR (P138) PEANUT BUTTER & MISO DIP WITH CINNAMON CRACKERS (P133)	PEANUT BUTTER & MISO DIP WITH CINNAMON CRACKERS (P133) TOASTED NORI CHIPS (P124)	SWEET POTATO ENERGY BALLS (P135) SENSATIONAL SEED CRACKERS (P145)

EATING PLAN TO CLEANSE

A meat-free, gluten-free and dairy-free plan designed for a short-term detox or to give your digestive system a break during times of stress.

	SUNDAY	MONDAY	TUESDAY	
WAKE UP	PINK DETOX TONIC (P27)	PINK DETOX TONIC (P27)	GLOWING SKIN TONIC (P24)	
BREAKFAST	BREKKIE VEGIE BURGER (P63)	GOODNESS SMOOTHIE BOWL (WITH COCONUT YOGHURT – SEE LORNA'S TIPS) (P52)	BAKED EGGS WITH KIMCHI (P66)	
LUNCH	CHILLI LENTIL VEGETABLE SOUP (WITHOUT PARMESAN – SEE LORNA'S TIPS) (P83)	EAT THE RAINBOW BOWL WITH CASHEW LEMON DRESSING (P92)	CRUNCHY SPROUT SALAD WITH SOFT-BOILED EGGS (P96)	
DINNER	PULLED FISH & SLAW TORTILLAS (P177)	GREEN MASALA VEGETABLE CURRY (SEE LORNA'S TIPS) (P191)	TOM YUM PRAWN BROCCOLI 'FRIED RICE' (P173)	
SNACKS	SWEET & SOUR ROASTED CHICKPEA & BEAN MIX (P141) SENSATIONAL SEED CRACKERS (P145)	BANANA, CHOC & PEANUT BUTTER WRAPS (P130) COCONUT YOGHURT (P129)	BEAT THE BLOAT SMOOTHIE (P36) SWEET & SOUR ROASTED CHICKPEA & BEAN MIX (P141)	

WEDNESDAY	THURSDAY	FRIDAY	SATURDAY
DIGESTIVE TONIC (P28)	PINK DETOX TONIC (P27)	CALM ME TONIC (P24)	DIGESTIVE TONIC (P28)
BLUEBERRY CHIA BIRCHER WITH CINNAMON GRANOLA (P42)	GOODNESS SMOOTHIE BOWL (WITH COCONUT YOGHURT – SEE LORNA'S TIPS) (P52)	COCONUT & APRICOT NO-GRAIN MUESLI WITH NUT MYLK (P55)	GREEN QUINOA WITH SESAME EGGS (P70)
CHILLI LENTIL VEGETABLE SOUP (WITHOUT PARMESAN – SEE LORNA'S TIPS) (P83)	PEA, MINT & MISO RICE PAPER ROLLS (P117)	ASIAN OMELETTE SALAD WITH WASABI DRESSING (WITHOUT CHICKEN – SEE LORNA'S TIPS) (P106)	CHILLI LENTIL VEGETABLE SOUP (WITHOUT PARMESAN – SEE LORNA'S TIPS) (P83)
PICK-YOUR-PROTEIN CURRY (TOFU) (P181)	SALMON WITH RED RICE, CABBAGE & TURMERIC DRESSING (P160)	ROAST SWEET POTATOES WITH CHILLI BLACK BEANS (P183)	POLENTA-CRUSTED FISH WITH PARSNIP MASH & SALSA (P174)
COCONUT YOGHURT (P129) SENSATIONAL SEED CRACKERS (P145)	SUPER GREEN SMOOTHIE (P39) SWEET & SOUR ROASTED CHICKPEA & BEAN MIX (P141)	SENSATIONAL SEED CRACKERS (P145) COCONUT YOGHURT (P129)	NUT & SEED BUTTER (P146) INCREDIBLE SEED BREAD (P149) WITH CASHEW BUTTER & KIWI (P151)

EATING PLAN FOR ENERGY

A plan to give you lots of energy. Perfect for those days or weeks when you have a busy schedule and need to be at your best.

□□□	SUNDAY	MONDAY	TUESDAY	
WAKE UP	POWER SEED SMOOTHIE (P36)	RECOVERY SMOOTHIE (P39)	BRAIN POWER SMOOTHIE (P35)	
BREAKFAST	OVERNIGHT OATS WITH BERRIES (P59)	OVERNIGHT OATS WITH BERRIES (P59)	MEXI-PROTEIN BEAN WRAPS (P60)	
LUNCH	WASABI CHICKEN WITH CUCUMBER & ASPARAGUS SALAD (P102)	SPEEDY COCONUT, HERB & PEA SOUP WITH CHICKEN (P80)	TEMPEH BLT SANDWICH (P109)	
DINNER	PICK-YOUR-PROTEIN CURRY (P181)	PULLED FISH & SLAW TORTILLAS (P177)	SPICED LAMB WITH MINT YOGHURT & QUINOA (P163)	
SNACKS	INCREDIBLE SEED BREAD (P149) SWEET POTATO ENERGY BALLS (P135)	INCREDIBLE SEED BREAD (P149) GREEN GODDESS MINI FRITTATAS (P142)	SWEET POTATO ENERGY BALLS (P135) COCONUT, PECAN & APRICOT BAR (P138)	

WEDNESDAY	THURSDAY	FRIDAY	SATURDAY
GREEN SUPER SMOOTHIE (P39)	BRAIN POWER SMOOTHIE (P35)	RECOVERY SMOOTHIE (P39)	GREEN SUPER SMOOTHIE (P39)
OVERNIGHT OATS WITH BERRIES (P59)	OMELETTE WITH WILTED KALE & GOAT'S CHEESE (P65)	OVERNIGHT OATS WITH BERRIES (P59)	SUPERFOOD BREKKIE BOWL (P76)
SALMON POKE BOWL (P105)	SPEEDY COCONUT, HERB & PEA SOUP WITH CHICKEN (P80)	EDAMAME FALAFEL WRAPS (P110)	PRAWN TACOS WITH CAULIFLOWER TORTILLAS (P113)
POACHED CHICKEN WITH AVOCADO & QUINOA SALAD (P168)	SALMON WITH ROASTED SPROUTS & CRISP CAPERS (P188)	SWEET POTATO FRITTATA (P178)	PARSNIP NOODLES WITH MEATBALLS (P184)
GREEN GODDESS MINI FRITTATAS (P142) SWEET POTATO ENERGY BALLS (P135)	AVOCADO BOATS WITH MISO SAUCE & CASHEWS (P120) COCONUT, PECAN & APRICOT BAR (P138)	INCREDIBLE SEED BREAD (P149) COCONUT, PECAN & APRICOT BAR (P138)	SENSATIONAL SEED CRACKERS (P145) NUT & SEED BUTTER (P146)

NOW JUST A LITTLE ON LIFESTYLE

Lifestyle factors can also have a direct effect on our overall wellbeing, and I believe that the amount of exercise we do, how we manage our stress, and how much sleep we get on a regular basis not only affects our ability to make good decisions when it comes to food, but also how we digest and absorb the nutrients from that food. It goes without saying that if you want to feel well – you need to eat well. So I've listed a few of the things I do on a regular basis to optimise my health and ensure that my body gets what it needs from the foods I eat.

I MANAGE MY STRESS

Stress is a modern-day reality for most of us – but did you know that when you're feeling overly-stressed (emotionally or physically) your stomach actually shuts down, making digestion and absorption of nutrients from your food almost impossible. Stress is also toxic for our immune system, and whilst it's almost impossible to completely eliminate stress from our lives, we can learn everyday-coping strategies that make it less impactful on our health.

When you're feeling a little stressed:

1. AID YOUR DIGESTION BY EATING MORE SLOWLY.

----

2. REDUCE YOUR INTAKE OF ANIMAL PRODUCTS AND GRAINS, AND CHOOSE TO EAT MORE SOUPS, SMOOTHIES, JUICES & TONICS.

----

3. INCREASE YOUR INTAKE OF VITAMIN C TO SUPPORT YOUR IMMUNE SYSTEM.

----

4. WHEN YOU'RE STRESSED YOUR BODY LOSES MAGNESIUM, SO TAKE A SUPPLEMENT, EAT FOODS HIGH IN MAGNESIUM OR HAVE AN EPSOM SALT BATH.

5. SIP CALMING TEAS SUCH AS CHAMOMILE OR PEPPERMINT.

----

6. SOAK IN A BATH WITH A LITTLE LAVENDER OIL ADDED. IT'S HARD TO HOLD ONTO STRESS WHEN YOU'RE SOAKING IN A RELAXING BATH.

----

7. PRACTISE YOGA REGULARLY.

----

8. TRY MEDITATING ONCE OR TWICE A DAY – I FIND THIS HELPS ME DEAL WITH ANY CHALLENGES I MIGHT FACE IN A BUSY DAY BY TEACHING MY MIND TO BE STILL.

I MOVE MY BODY EVERY DAY

REGULAR EXERCISE DOES SO MUCH MORE THAN JUST KEEP YOU FIT. IT IMPROVES CIRCULATION AND GETS THE BLOOD MOVING THROUGH YOUR BODY TO SPEED UP THE DELIVERY OF NUTRIENTS FROM YOUR FOOD TO EXACTLY WHERE YOUR BODY NEEDS THEM. EXERCISE ALSO AIDS DETOXIFICATION AND LYMPHATIC DRAINAGE. YOU'LL HAVE BETTER SLEEP, FEEL GREAT, HAVE MORE CONFIDENCE AND, BEST OF ALL, LIVE LONGER.

I PROTECT MY SLEEP

Sleep is just as important for your
health as nutrition and fitness –
because it gives your body time to
repair its muscles, create new tissue,
build protein and release human
growth hormone.

I think of my sleep as restorative
time for my mind and body because
I know that getting enough of it
is the best way to maximise the
benefits of my nutrition. Sleep
also improves my mood, lifts my
concentration, helps me look and
feel younger, and, believe it or not,
stay in shape!

*Here are some of the things I do
to protect my sleep:*

1. I prioritise it, aiming for
7–9 hours every night.
2. I don't have caffeinated
drinks (or foods) past 11am.
3. I use soft lighting in my
bedroom, keep it cool in temperature
and free from electronic devices.
4. I keep the same wake-up
time every day and aim for
roughly the same bedtime to get
my body into a good routine.
5. If I'm having difficulty sleeping,
I try to wind down with some
yoga stretches, a nice warm bath
or a calming tea.

TONICS & SMOOTHIES

What you feed yourself today can change your tomorrow –
and what better way to give yourself a nutritious boost any time
of the day than with a health-promoting tonic or smoothie.
I am constantly amazed at the power of food and these delicious
blends are a daily ritual for me. I have one as soon as I wake up to
kickstart my morning workout and then another in the afternoon
to keep my focus and energy levels high. The recipes in this book
are ones that I have experimented with over time – and I can
honestly say they're delicious. So whether you're looking for a
little more energy, some brain power, glowing skin or to simply
get rid of that bloated feeling! – I'm sure that once you experience
the many benefits of these nutrient-packed beverages,
they'll quickly become a non-negotiable part of your day too.

Calm Me
TONIC

PREP + COOK TIME 25 MINUTES
(+ STANDING & REFRIGERATION)
MAKES 1 LITRE (4 CUPS) SERVES 4

1.25 litres (5 cups) water
⅓ cup dried chamomile flowers
  (or 3 tea bags)
¼ cup lemon thyme sprigs
4 slices lemon
1 tablespoon pure maple syrup

1 Bring water to boil in a medium saucepan; remove from heat. Add chamomile, lemon thyme and lemon slices. Stir in maple syrup. Cover; stand for 20 minutes. Strain tea; discard solids.

2 Refrigerate for at least 1 hour or until cooled. Serve tea mixture over ice with extra lemon thyme sprigs, if you like.

NUTRITIONAL COUNT PER SERVING protein (0.1g); carbohydrate (4.7g); total fat (0.1g); fibre (0g)

Chamomile tea is known for its calming effect, making this the perfect soothing and relaxing tonic.

Glowing Skin
TONIC

PREP TIME 5 MINUTES
MAKES 2 CUPS (500ML) SERVES 2

2 medium carrots (240g), unpeeled,
  chopped coarsely
4 medium oranges (960g), peeled,
  chopped coarsely
15g (½oz) fresh turmeric, unpeeled

1 Push carrot, orange and turmeric through a juice extractor into a jug. Stir to combine.

2 Serve straight away with crushed ice, ribbons of extra carrot and strips of orange rind, if you like.

NUTRITIONAL COUNT PER SERVING protein (3.2g); carbohydrate (21g); total fat (2.2g); fibre (1.8g)

LORNA'S TIPS Turmeric is strongly coloured and can stain your hands and chopping boards, so line boards with baking paper and wear plastic gloves. The juice will separate on standing; however, a quick stir will bring it back together.

Oranges, carrots, turmeric and pepper all contain anti-inflammatory antioxidants.

PINK DETOX *Tonic*

PREP TIME 10 MINUTES MAKES 400ML SERVES 4

250g (8oz) strawberries, hulled
1 tablespoon lemon juice
¼ teaspoon ground cinnamon
½ cup (125ml) filtered water
1 cup crushed ice (optional)

1 Blend strawberries, juice, cinnamon and water in a high-powered blender until smooth.

2 Divide ice and tonic between glasses. Serve straight away with extra strawberries, if you like.

NUTRITIONAL COUNT PER SERVING protein (1.1g); carbohydrate (2g); total fat (0.1g); fibre (1g)

LORNA'S TIP All the ingredients in this tonic have detoxifying properties; however, for an extra detox boost, add 1 teaspoon activated charcoal to each serve. Activated charcoal is available from health food stores.

When ingested, activated charcoal aids digestion, improves immunity and absorbs and removes toxins from the digestive tract – use in moderation and always 2 hours before taking any medication or vitamins to avoid interference.

Digestive
TONIC

PREP TIME 5 MINUTES
(+ 1 WEEK STANDING)
MAKES 2 CUPS (500ML) SERVES 12

1 baby fennel bulb (130g)
1 teaspoon fennel seeds
2 tablespoons raw honey
2 tablespoons raw sugar
2 cups (500ml) apple cider vinegar
  with the mother (see Lorna's Tips)
ice cubes & chilled sparkling water

1 Thinly slice fennel bulb, reserving the
fronds, if you like. Combine sliced fennel,
fennel seeds, honey and sugar in a sterilised
3-cup (750ml) capacity jar. (For tips on how
to sterilise, see page 246.) Pour vinegar over
the fennel mixture. Seal jar; store in a dark,
cool place for 1 week. Strain the vinegar
into a clean jar.

2 Just before serving, place 2 tablespoons
of the vinegar tonic in a glass with ice cubes;
top up each glass with ¾ cup (180ml)
sparkling water. Serve with fennel fronds,
if you like.

NUTRITIONAL COUNT PER SERVING protein (0.1g);
carbohydrate (6g); total fat (0g); fibre (0g)

LORNA'S TIPS The fermenting process of this
tonic takes 1 week (but trust me, it's worth
the wait). Apple cider vinegar with the
mother is available from health food stores
and major supermarkets. Tonic will last for
a year in a cool, dark place.

*Apple cider vinegar with the mother contains
enzymes and bacteria that are great for your
gut health.*

Metabolism Boosting
TONIC

PREP + COOK TIME 5 MINUTES
(+ REFRIGERATION)
MAKES 1 LITRE (4 CUPS) SERVES 4

1 peppermint tea bag
1 cup (250ml) boiling water
800g (1½lb) chopped watermelon
2 medium limes (180g), peeled
½ cup (125ml) chilled aloe vera juice
1½ tablespoons white chia seeds

1 Place tea bag and the boiling water in
a large heatproof jug; stand for 2 minutes.
Discard tea bag. Refrigerate for 1 hour or
until cold.

2 Push watermelon and limes through a
juice extractor into a jug. Add to chilled tea
with aloe vera juice and chia seeds; stir to
combine. Refrigerate for at least 15 minutes
or until seeds have swollen and softened.

3 Serve with extra watermelon wedges and
slices of lime, if you like.

NUTRITIONAL COUNT PER SERVING protein (2g);
carbohydrate (15g); total fat (2.9g);
fibre (1.4g)

LORNA'S TIP This tonic will keep in the fridge
for 24 hours; stir before serving.

*Peppermint tea is good for digestion, while
aloe vera helps with bloating. Chia seeds are
packed with fibre to keep you feeling full for
longer, and watermelon is super hydrating
and anti-inflammatory.*

GINGER *Kombucha* (FOR IMMUNITY & DIGESTION)

PREP + COOK TIME 15 MINUTES (+ 7–14 DAYS FERMENTING) MAKES 800ML SERVES 8

2 tablespoons loose-leaf organic green tea

½ cup (125ml) pure maple syrup

1 litre (4 cups) filtered water, boiling

1 kombucha SCOBY 'mother' (see Buying)

¼ cup (60ml) kombucha starter liquid (see Buying)

½ cup (50g) ginger, peeled, chopped into 3cm (1¼in) pieces

½ cup (125ml) lemon juice

1 Sterilise a wide-mouth 2-litre (8-cup) glass jar. (For tips on how to sterilise, see page 246.)

2 Place tea and maple syrup in sterilised jar. Pour the boiling water on top and stir until combined. Cover; stand at room temperature overnight to brew.

3 Using a sieve lined with cheesecloth, strain tea into a 1-litre (4-cup) capacity jug (discard the tea leaves).

4 Rewash and sterilise the jar; leave to cool. Pour cooled tea into sterilised jar.

5 Using food-handling gloves, carefully place the SCOBY 'mother' on top of the tea and pour over starter liquid. Cover the top of the jar with two layers of cheesecloth; secure with a rubber band. Stand at a stable cool room temperature (away from direct sunlight) for 7–14 days or until fermented. The fermented kombucha will have a slightly vinegary flavour and an almost pungent aroma. The length of time the kombucha takes to brew will depend on the temperature: in summer, it will ferment much faster than in winter.

6 Pour kombucha into a 1-litre (4-cup) capacity glass bottle with a lid; leave the SCOBY and ¼ cup of the liquid in the jar to make another batch (see below). Stir ginger and lemon juice into kombucha. Refrigerate until chilled, or allow kombucha to stand at a stable cool room temperature for 12 hours, or until bubbles start forming, then refrigerate.

BUYING SCOBY (or starter kits, as they are commonly called) are available online. A SCOBY will make the mother and starter liquid. When handling a SCOBY 'mother', don't use metal utensils; use plastic utensils or wear food-handling gloves. The SCOBY we used in this recipe was 3mm (⅛ in) thick.

NUTRITIONAL COUNT PER SERVING protein (0.3g); carbohydrate (14.1g); total fat (0.2g); fibre (0g)

LORNA'S TIP You will need to start this recipe 8–15 days ahead (so that the sugars can be broken down by the fermenting process).

MAKING A SECOND BATCH Using the SCOBY and liquid left in the jar, repeat the recipe. If you want to take a break, cover the jar containing the SCOBY and liquid with cheesecloth and secure with a rubber band; stand at a stable cool room temperature (away from direct sunlight) for 7 days.

FLAVOUR VARIATION Passionfruit: Omit ginger and add the pulp of 6 passionfruit (½ cup).

Kombucha is a lightly effervescent drink rich in probiotics and made from sweetened tea fermented by bacteria and yeast (known as a SCOBY, or a symbiotic colony of bacteria and yeast). It helps replenish your gut bacteria and supports digestion.

Discover the power of food — because what you eat lays the foundation for how you feel every day.

Brain Power

SMOOTHIE

PREP TIME 10 MINUTES SERVES 2

1 cup (250ml) canned coconut milk
1 cup (150g) frozen blueberries
1 small beetroot (beet) (100g),
    washed, grated
2 tablespoons cacao powder

1 Blend ingredients in a high-powered blender until smooth. Adjust the consistency by adding extra coconut milk, if necessary.

2 Serve topped with a few extra blueberries, if you like.

NUTRITIONAL COUNT PER SERVING protein (5.4g); carbohydrate (15.3g); total fat (21.2g); fibre (3.3g)

LORNA'S TIP Make this smoothie in advance and keep it in the fridge in a sealed jar for an afternoon brain-power lift. Stir or shake to bring it back together.

Antioxidant-rich blueberries stimulate the flow of blood and oxygen to the brain. Similarly, the nitrates in beetroot encourage blood flow to the brain. Flavanol-rich cacao protects the brain from toxins and inflammation.

De-stress

SMOOTHIE

PREP TIME 5 MINUTES SERVES 2

¼ cup (40g) blanched almonds
¾ cup (180ml) water
1 large orange (300g)
2 small fresh figs (100g), chopped
1 tablespoon vanilla protein powder
    (see Lorna's Tips)
1 tablespoon hulled tahini
1 tablespoon chia seeds

1 Blend almonds and water in a high-powered blender until smooth.

2 Peel orange and chop flesh. Add orange and remaining ingredients to blender; blend until smooth.

3 Serve in jars or glasses with orange rind and extra fresh figs, if you like.

NUTRITIONAL COUNT PER SERVING protein (12.8g); carbohydrate (13g); total fat (20.6g); fibre (9.4g)

LORNA'S TIPS The almonds and water will make 1 cup (250ml) almond mylk, which can also be used in other smoothie recipes. You can use purchased almond mylk, if you prefer. If you are opting for a dairy-free smoothie, then choose a vegan protein powder, such as pea or brown rice protein. If dairy is not an issue, use a whey protein powder.

Tahini and chia seeds both contain serotonin-releasing magnesium and tryptophan, an amino acid that lifts your mood and promotes good sleep, as well as mood-boosting omega-3s.

Beat the Bloat

SMOOTHIE

PREP TIME 10 MINUTES SERVES 2

⅓ cup (45g) raw macadamias or cashews
1¼ cups (310ml) water
2 large bananas (460g), chopped coarsely,
  frozen
1 tablespoon cacao powder
1 tablespoon chia seeds
1 tablespoon tahini
1 teaspoon maca powder
1 teaspoon ground cardamom

1 Blend nuts and water in a high-powered blender until smooth. Add frozen banana along with remaining ingredients; blend until smooth.

2 Serve straight away, dusted with a little extra cacao powder, if you like.

NUTRITIONAL COUNT PER SERVING protein (9.2g); carbohydrate (39.8g); total fat (29.1g); fibre (9.2g)

LORNA'S TIPS You can use 1½ cups (375ml) almond mylk instead of the nuts and water, if you prefer. If you would like to create a striped effect in your glass, blend 2 teaspoons cacoa powder and 3 teaspoons maple syrup to form a paste. Spread paste around the inside top of each glass. This is not included in the nutrition count.

If you know that you suffer from menstrual cramps, make this smoothie in the week leading up to your period as a preventative.

Power Seed

SMOOTHIE

PREP TIME 5 MINUTES SERVES 2

1 small banana (130g), chopped coarsely,
  frozen
1 cup (280g) kefir yoghurt or Greek-style
  yoghurt (see Lorna's Tips)
⅓ cup (80ml) water
1 cup (150g) frozen mixed berries
1 tablespoon dried cherries or cranberries
1 tablespoon pure maple syrup
1 teaspoon linseeds (flaxseeds)
1 teaspoon chia seeds

1 Blend frozen banana with remaining ingredients in a high-powered blender until smooth. Add a little extra water, if needed.

2 Serve straight away, topped with cherry powder (see Lorna's Tips) and extra chia seeds and dried cherries, if you like.

NUTRITIONAL COUNT PER SERVING protein (9.4g); carbohydrate (45.9g); total fat (10.2g); fibre (5.3g)

LORNA'S TIPS Kefir yoghurt is available from major supermarkets and health food stores; alternatively, use 1½ cups (375ml) kefir yoghurt drink or almond mylk and drop the water. To make cherry powder, blend or process some dried cherries to a powder.

Super Green

SMOOTHIE

PREP TIME 10 MINUTES SERVES 2

1 cup (250ml) coconut water
200g (6½oz) frozen pineapple
  (see Lorna's Tip)
½ small avocado (100g)
¼ baby fennel bulb (35g)
¼ cup loosely packed mint leaves
1 cup firmly packed baby spinach leaves
1 tablespoon lime juice
1 cup ice cubes (optional)

1 Blend all ingredients except the ice
in a high-powered blender until smooth.

2 Serve straight away over ice, topped
with extra mint leaves, if you like.

NUTRITIONAL COUNT PER SERVING protein (2.8g);
carbohydrate (15.3g); total fat (7.4g);
fibre (3.6g)

LORNA'S TIP Frozen pineapple is available
from supermarkets, or you can freeze your
own peeled, cored, chopped and portioned
pineapple in small containers.

*This smoothie is the perfect all-rounder – with
pineapple for vitamin C, spinach for iron and
antioxidants, avocado for healthy fats and
fennel to aid digestion.*

Recovery

SMOOTHIE

PREP TIME 5 MINUTES SERVES 2

¼ cup (35g) raw macadamias or cashews
¾ cup (180ml) water
1 tablespoon vanilla-flavoured
  protein powder
2 tablespoons almond butter
½ medium ripe avocado (125g)
2 teaspoons pure maple syrup
½ medium banana (100g)
1 cup ice cubes (optional)

1 Blend nuts and the water in a
high-powered blender until smooth.

2 Add remaining ingredients except
ice. Blend for 1 minute or until smooth.

3 Serve straight away over ice, if you like.

NUTRITIONAL COUNT PER SERVING protein (8.1g);
carbohydrate (21.1g); total fat (32.5g);
fibre (4.6g)

LORNA'S TIP You can use 1 cup (250ml) of
almond mylk instead of the nuts and water.

*This high-protein smoothie is the perfect
post-workout drink to help kickstart your
body's recovery.*

WAKE UP

Breakfast is without doubt the most important meal of the day —
and while a busy world might tempt us to skip it from time to
time, we need to remind ourselves that what we choose to eat
in the morning really does set us up for the rest of our day.
I'm a huge fan of breakfast foods — not only because they're
delicious but because I know that giving my body a nutrient-
boost in the morning really does kickstart my metabolism,
boost my energy levels and put me in a good mood.
The following recipes would have to be some of my favourite
ways to start the day. And you'll never want to skip breakfast
again with so many delicious options that you can prepare ahead
of time to grab and go, and others that are perfect to enjoy with
family and friends when you have a little more time.

BLUEBERRY CHIA BIRCHER WITH
Cinnamon Granola

PREP + COOK TIME 25 MINUTES (+ OVERNIGHT REFRIGERATION) SERVES 4

250g (8oz) fresh blueberries

2 cups (560g) Greek-style yoghurt

¼ cup (40g) white chia seeds

½ teaspoon pure vanilla extract

1 tablespoon pure maple syrup

¾ cup (60g) traditional rolled oats

½ cup (40g) raw almonds,
  chopped coarsely

½ teaspoon ground cinnamon

⅓ cup (50g) pomegranate seeds

1 Reserve a quarter of the blueberries. Mash remaining berries in a bowl with yoghurt until combined. Add chia seeds, vanilla and 2 teaspoons of the maple syrup. Cover; refrigerate overnight.

2 Preheat oven to 200°C/400°F.

3 To make granola, place oats on an oven tray. Bake for 5 minutes or until oats are lightly browned. Add almonds, cinnamon and remaining maple syrup; mix well. Bake for another 5 minutes or until almonds are golden. Cool.

4 Spoon the yoghurt mixture into four 1-cup (250ml) cups or bowls. Top with granola, pomegranate seeds and reserved berries.

NUTRITIONAL COUNT PER SERVING protein (13.1g); carbohydrate (40.8g); total fat (19.5g); fibre (7g)

MAKE & STASH Make a double batch of the granola and store in an airtight container for up to 2 weeks.

Blueberries are packed with anthocyanins and are an excellent source of vitamin C. A half cup of blueberries has the same amount of fibre as a slice of wholegrain bread.

CINNAMON & VANILLA
Brown Rice Porridge

PREP + COOK TIME 50 MINUTES SERVES 6

1¼ cups (250g) brown rice

¾ cup (65g) rolled oats

1.25 litres (5 cups) water

1 cinnamon stick, halved

½ vanilla bean, split, seeds scraped

½ teaspoon sea salt flakes

½ cup (125ml) almond mylk

2 medium bananas (400g), sliced

250g (8oz) strawberries, sliced

¼ cup (35g) roasted hazelnuts,
    chopped

¾ cup (200g) coconut yoghurt

2 tablespoons pure maple syrup

pinch ground cinnamon

1 Combine rice, oats, water, cinnamon stick, vanilla bean and seeds, and salt in a medium saucepan over high heat; bring to boil. Reduce heat to low; simmer, covered, for 40 minutes, stirring occasionally to prevent sticking to the base of the pan, or until grains are tender with a slight bite.

2 Stir in mylk; cook, stirring, for 5 minutes or until heated through.

3 Serve porridge topped with fruit, hazelnuts and yoghurt; drizzle with maple syrup and sprinkle with ground cinnamon. Discard vanilla bean and cinnamon stick.

NUTRITIONAL COUNT PER SERVING protein (9g); carbohydrate (60.4g); total fat (9.9g); fibre (5.3g)

LORNA'S TIP You can make the porridge the night before to save time. Add a little more water or almond mylk on reheating.

PEPITA, ALMOND & PEAR *Muffins*

PREP + COOK TIME 40 MINUTES MAKES 12

¼ cup (35g) sulphite-free dried
  cherries or cranberries
2 tablespoons water
½ cup (100g) pepitas
  (pumpkin seed kernels)
½ cup (80g) natural almonds,
  chopped coarsely
1¼ cups (160g) wholemeal plain
  (all-purpose) spelt flour
  (see Lorna's Tip)
2½ teaspoons baking powder
  (see Lorna's Tip)
½ cup (140g) Greek-style yoghurt
2 teaspoons grated orange rind
½ cup (125ml) orange juice
¼ cup (60ml) pure maple syrup
1 free-range egg
¼ cup (60ml) cold-pressed
  extra-virgin olive oil
1 small pear (180g), chopped finely

1 Preheat oven to 180°C/350°F. Line a 12-hole
(⅓-cup/80ml) muffin pan with paper cases.

2 Place cherries in a small bowl with the water;
stand for 10 minutes. Drain any water left from
the cherries. Combine pepitas and almonds in
a small bowl.

3 Sift flour and baking powder into a large bowl;
return husks to bowl. Add cherries and half the nut
mix to the bowl. Whisk yoghurt, rind, juice, maple
syrup, egg and oil in a jug; pour into flour mixture
and stir until just combined. Fold in the pear.

4 Spoon mixture into paper cases; sprinkle with
remaining nut mix.

5 Bake muffins for 18 minutes or until a skewer
inserted into the centre comes out clean.

NUTRITIONAL COUNT PER MUFFIN protein (6.1g);
carbohydrate (20.6g); total fat (13.4g); fibre (3.2g)

LORNA'S TIP If you can find self-raising wholemeal
spelt flour, leave out the baking powder.

MAKE & STASH Muffins can be frozen individually
for up to 2 months; thaw overnight and reheat
for a quick breakfast.

Eating breakfast sets you up for success —
it fuels your body, giving you increased energy and mental focus.

MANGO LASSI WHIP WITH
Pistachio Crumble

PREP + COOK TIME 15 MINUTES SERVES 4

1⅔ cups (400g) coconut kefir yoghurt
  or Greek-style yoghurt
2 cups (300g) frozen diced mango
¼ cup (60ml) pure maple syrup
¼ teaspoon ground turmeric
2 passionfruit, halved
½ cup (25g) flaked coconut, toasted

PISTACHIO CRUMBLE
½ cup (45g) rolled oats
2 tablespoons pistachios,
  chopped coarsely
1 tablespoon pure maple syrup
1 tablespoon cold-pressed
  extra-virgin coconut oil, melted
½ teaspoon ground cardamom

1 To make pistachio crumble, combine ingredients in a small bowl. Heat a large heavy-based frying pan over medium heat. Cook oat mixture, stirring with a wooden spoon, for 3 minutes or until toasted and golden brown. Remove from heat; cool in pan.

2 To make lassi whip, blend yoghurt, frozen mango, maple syrup and turmeric until smooth.

3 Divide lassi whip among glasses. Top with passionfruit, flaked coconut and pistachio crumble.

NUTRITIONAL COUNT PER SERVING protein (5.1g); carbohydrate (37.9g); total fat (29g); fibre (4.9g)

LORNA'S TIP If you'd like to make this ahead, pour mango lassi whip into a 1-litre (4-cup) loaf pan or freezer-safe container; cover surface closely with plastic wrap. Freeze for 4 hours or overnight. Remove from freezer for 10 minutes to soften slightly before scooping, then blend to a slushie consistency.

GOODNESS *Smoothie Bowl*

PREP TIME 10 MINUTES (+ FREEZING) SERVES 4

2 medium bananas (400g),
   sliced thinly

1 ripe medium avocado (250g),
   chopped

250g (8oz) strawberries

2 kiwifruit (170g)

1 cup (100g) chopped
   raw cauliflower

2 tablespoons pure maple syrup

1 medium ripe pear (230g),
   unpeeled, cored, chopped

²/₃ cup baby spinach leaves

1 cup (280g) kefir yoghurt or
   Greek-style yoghurt

2 tablespoons lime juice

¼ cup (60ml) canned coconut milk
   (see Lorna's Tips)

½ cup ice cubes

¼ cup (20g) shredded coconut

1 tablespoon chia seeds

1 Place banana and avocado in a large resealable bag. Freeze for at least 20 minutes, but no more than 40 minutes, while preparing remaining ingredients.

2 Meanwhile, slice strawberries and kiwifruit.

3 Blend frozen avocado and banana, cauliflower, maple syrup, pear, spinach, yoghurt, lime juice, coconut milk and ice cubes in a high-powered blender until smooth. Taste for sweetness, as this may vary depending on ripeness of fruit; adjust to taste with extra maple syrup, if you like.

4 Divide the smoothie mixture among bowls. Top with strawberry and kiwi slices, shredded coconut and chia seeds. Serve straight away.

NUTRITIONAL COUNT PER SERVING protein (9.1g); carbohydrate (48.7g); total fat (19.5g); fibre (9.2g)

LORNA'S TIPS If you don't want to open a can of coconut milk, use extra kefir yoghurt instead. For the Eating Plan to Cleanse on pages 16–17, swap the kefir or Greek-style yoghurt for a dairy-free alternative such as coconut yoghurt.

1

2

Muesli

3

COCONUT & APRICOT NO-GRAIN MUESLI

PREP + COOK TIME 15 MINUTES MAKES 5 CUPS

Preheat oven to 180°C/350°F. Line an oven tray with baking paper. Combine 1 cup (50g) flaked coconut and 1 cup (130g) natural seed mix that includes pine nuts on tray. Using a zesting tool, remove rind from 1 medium orange (or finely grate) and combine with nut mixture. Bake for 8 minutes, stirring halfway through, or until nuts are toasted. Cool. Stir in 3 cups (40g) puffed buckwheat and ½ cup (75g) chopped sulphite-free dried apricots.

CACAO POPS

PREP + COOK TIME 20 MINUTES MAKES 1¼ CUPS

Preheat oven to 180°C/350°F. Line a large oven tray with baking paper. Combine 1 cup (20g) puffed millet, 1 tablespoon cacao powder, 1½ tablespoons pure maple syrup, ¼ teaspoon sea salt flakes and ⅓ cup (45g) coarsely chopped hazelnuts in a bowl until millet is well coated. Spoon in clumps onto tray. Bake, turning once, for 15 minutes or until crisp. Cool.

WINTER SPICE MUESLI

PREP + COOK TIME 25 MINUTES MAKES 3½ CUPS

Preheat oven to 180°C/350°F. Line an oven tray with baking paper. Place 2 cups (180g) rolled oats and 1 cup (100g) chopped walnuts on tray. Sift over 1½ teaspoons mixed spice. Coarsely grate 1 medium (150g) red-skinned apple over oat mixture on tray. Drizzle with 1 tablespoon cold-pressed extra-virgin olive oil. Mix until well coated. Bake for 20 minutes or until toasted. Cool; stir in ½ cup (65g) dried cranberries.

LORNA'S TIP Use dried fruit without added sulphites, sugar or colouring.

MAKE & STASH Store muesli in an airtight container for up to 2 weeks.

CHIA SPELT CRÊPES WITH
Caramelised Peaches

PREP + COOK TIME 25 MINUTES (+ STANDING) SERVES 4

¾ cup (110g) wholemeal plain
  (all-purpose) spelt flour
1 tablespoon white chia seeds
2½ tablespoons pure maple sugar
½ teaspoon ground cinnamon
1 cup (250ml) almond mylk
½ cup (125ml) water, approximately
1½ tablespoons cold-pressed
  extra-virgin coconut oil, melted
4 peaches (600g), halved
⅔ cup (190g) coconut yoghurt
  (see page 129)
2 tablespoons roasted flaked almonds
1 tablespoon pure maple syrup

1 Combine flour, chia seeds, 2 teaspoons of the maple sugar and the cinnamon in a medium bowl. Make a well in the centre, then gradually whisk in combined almond mylk and the water until smooth. Stand for 20 minutes.

2 Heat a 26cm (10½in) (top measurement) non-stick frying pan over high heat. Lightly grease with some of the oil. Pour ½ cup of the batter into the centre of the hot pan, tilting pan to coat the base in a thin layer; cook for 1 minute or until browned. Turn and cook on the other side until golden. Transfer to a plate; cover to keep warm. Repeat with remaining batter, greasing pan with oil, to make a total of 4 crêpes.

3 Reduce heat to medium-high. Sprinkle remaining sugar on cut side of peach halves. Cook peaches in pan, cut-side down, for 1 minute or until lightly caramelised. Cut half of the peach halves into 3 wedges each.

4 Divide crêpes among plates. Top with peaches, yoghurt, almonds and maple syrup.

NUTRITIONAL COUNT PER SERVING protein (9.5g); carbohydrate (47.6g); total fat (26.3g); fibre (8.5g)

LORNA'S TIPS The hotter the pan the better the crêpes will be; however, remove the pan from the heat for a few seconds between making each crêpe so they don't burn. You can also make this recipe with finger bananas, figs, cherries or other stone fruit, depending on what is the ripest and nicest.

OVERNIGHT OATS WITH *Berries*

PREP + COOK TIME 15 MINUTES (+ OVERNIGHT REFRIGERATION) SERVES 4

5 medium green-skinned apples
   (750g)
2 cups (180g) rolled oats
1 cup (250ml) almond mylk
250g (8oz) strawberries
1 tablespoon pure maple syrup
125g (4oz) raspberries,
   fresh or frozen

1 Push 3 apples through a juice extractor; you will need 1 cup of juice.

2 Place oats, mylk and apple juice in a large bowl; stir to combine. Cover; refrigerate overnight.

3 Coarsely grate 1 apple. Cut remaining apple into matchsticks. Fold grated apple into oat mixture.

4 Quarter 2 strawberries and slice 2 strawberries; reserve to serve. Slice remaining strawberries and place in a medium bowl. Using a wooden spoon, smash strawberries until crushed coarsely. Stir in maple syrup.

5 Layer the muddled strawberries, half the raspberries and the oat mixture in a shallow serving dish or four bowls, finishing with some of the strawberries. Serve topped with apple matchsticks, reserved strawberries and remaining raspberries.

NUTRITIONAL COUNT PER SERVING protein (8.8g); carbohydrate (48.8g); total fat (11g); fibre (9.8g)

LORNA'S TIP Instead of making your own apple juice, use a purchased cloudy apple juice, if you prefer.

MAKE & STASH Make double the oat mixture to eat throughout the week; store in an airtight container in the fridge for up to 5 days. Layer with different fruits each day.

You will need to start this recipe the night before.

MEXI-PROTEIN *Bean Wraps*

PREP + COOK TIME 20 MINUTES MAKES 4

400g (12½oz) cherry truss tomatoes

¼ cup (60ml) cold-pressed
   extra-virgin olive oil

400g (12½oz) can black beans,
   drained, rinsed

2 tablespoons water

2 teaspoons cumin seeds

8 free-range eggs, whisked,
   seasoned

1 large avocado (320g), chopped

8 small stone-ground blue corn
   tortillas (200g), warmed
   (see Lorna's Tip)

⅓ cup coriander (cilantro) leaves

1 jalapeño chilli, chopped finely

1 tablespoon lime juice

chipotle pepper sauce or
   green tabasco, to serve (optional)

1 Preheat oven to 180°C/350°F. Line an oven tray
with baking paper.

2 Place tomatoes on tray; drizzle with 1 tablespoon
of the oil. Season; bake for 15 minutes or until
tomatoes start to soften.

3 Meanwhile, combine beans and water in
a small saucepan; cook, covered, over low heat,
for 5 minutes or until heated through. Drain.

4 Heat 2 teaspoons of the oil in a large heavy-based
frying pan over medium heat. Add cumin seeds and
cook for 1 minute or until starting to crackle.
Add egg; cook, stirring gently, until just starting
to set. Remove from heat.

5 Divide beans, scrambled egg and avocado among
tortillas; scatter with coriander. Season to taste.

6 Combine chilli, lime juice and remaining oil
in a small bowl; drizzle over filling. Serve with
tomatoes, lime cheeks and hot sauce, if you like.

NUTRITIONAL COUNT PER WRAP protein (12.9g);
carbohydrate (16g); total fat (19.6g); fibre (5.8g)

LORNA'S TIP Stoneground blue corn tortillas are
available from some health food stores. You can
use multigrain or corn tortillas if not available.

BREKKIE Vegie Burger

PREP + COOK TIME 40 MINUTES MAKES 2

4 x 100g (3oz) large portobello
 mushrooms, trimmed

2 tablespoons cold-pressed
 extra-virgin olive oil

4 slices eggplant (150g)

100g (3oz) tofu, cut into 2 slabs
 crossways

1 tablespoon dukkah

200g (6½oz) tomatoes, sliced thickly

2 teaspoons apple cider vinegar

¼ cup (35g) drained semi-dried
 tomatoes

½ cup (140g) Greek-style yoghurt

½ small avocado (100g), sliced thinly

50g (1½oz) rocket (arugula)

1 Preheat oven to 200°C/400°F. Line a large oven tray with baking paper.

2 Place mushrooms, cup-side up, on tray; drizzle with 2 teaspoons of the oil and season. Place eggplant and tofu on tray; drizzle with 1 tablespoon of oil and scatter tofu with dukkah. Roast vegetables and tofu for 25 minutes or until tender.

3 Meanwhile, toss tomato in remaining oil and vinegar in a medium bowl.

4 Process semi-dried tomatoes and yoghurt in a small food processor until smooth. Season to taste.

5 Place two mushrooms, cup-side up, on plates. Top each with a slice of eggplant, tofu, tomato, avocado, rocket, yoghurt sauce, remaining eggplant slice and remaining mushroom, cup-side down. Season to taste. Serve with red-vein sorrel leaves, if you like.

NUTRITIONAL COUNT PER BURGER protein (22.2g); carbohydrate (23.5g); total fat (37.3g); fibre (13.5g)

LORNA'S TIP Yoghurt sauce can be made a day ahead; keep tightly covered in the fridge.

1

QUICK
& EASY
Omelettes

2

BASIC OMELETTE

PREP + COOK TIME 10 MINUTES SERVES 2

Beat 4 free-range eggs and 2 tablespoons water in a bowl with a fork until combined. Season. Heat a small frying pan over medium-high heat. Add 1 teaspoon cold-pressed extra-virgin olive oil, then half the egg mixture. Using a wide spatula, gently push the set egg mixture towards the centre of pan, tilting the pan to spread out the mixture until egg is almost set. Top with your desired filling. Fold one side of the omelette over using the spatula. Slide onto a plate. Repeat.

Filling variations

PEA, MINT & RICOTTA

Drop ½ cup (80g) fresh or frozen peas into a small pan of boiling water; simmer until just tender, then drain. Place in a bowl and mash with a fork. Season. Divide peas between omelettes; sprinkle with ¼ cup (60g) crumbled ricotta and ¼ cup mint sprigs.

TOMATO & BASIL

Seed and chop 1 large heirloom tomato. Divide tomato and 2 tablespoons shredded basil leaves between omelettes. Season. Sprinkle with extra basil leaves.

KALE & GOAT'S CHEESE

Heat 2 teaspoons cold-pressesd extra-virgin olive oil in a frying pan. Add 1 small sliced clove garlic and 2 cups loosely packed baby kale; cook, stirring, until wilted. Season. Divide kale between omelettes and sprinkle with 60g (2oz) crumbled goat's cheese. Sprinkle with extra baby kale.

BAKED EGGS WITH *Kimchi*

PREP + COOK TIME 25 MINUTES SERVES 4

1⅓ cups (300g) kimchi

200g (6½oz) canned diced tomatoes
   (see Lorna's Tips)

4 free-range eggs

4 slices sourdough bread (160g)

½ cup (40g) bean sprouts

½ cup (40g) crunchy combo sprouts
   (see Lorna's Tips)

¼ cup coriander (cilantro) leaves

¼ cup mint leaves

1   Preheat oven to 220°C/425°F.

2   Divide kimchi and tomatoes between four ovenproof bowls or dishes. Make an indent in the kimchi mixture; carefully break an egg into each indent. Wrap each bowl in baking paper and tie with string, or cover with a lid or foil. Bake for 15 minutes or until egg whites are just set.

3   Meanwhile, toast sourdough bread on heated grill plate.

4   Top each bowl with sprouts and herbs. Serve with toasted sourdough.

NUTRITIONAL COUNT PER SERVING protein (15.6g); carbohydrate (21.2g); total fat (6.6g); fibre (6.6g)

LORNA'S TIPS Choose canned tomatoes with no added sugar. You can freeze remaining canned tomatoes in a container for up to 3 months. Crunchy combo sprouts are made from sprouted legumes such as mung beans, peas and lentils. They are available fresh in supermarkets and grocery stores.

Kimchi is a traditional Korean fermented cabbage dish found in Asian supermarkets that is great for gut health.

MUSHROOM & LABNE *French Toast*

PREP + COOK TIME 20 MINUTES SERVES 2

2 free-range eggs

½ cup (125ml) almond mylk

2 teaspoons dijon mustard

2 tablespoons finely grated
  parmesan

4 slices sourdough or
  grainy bread (120g)

2 tablespoons cold-pressed
  extra-virgin olive oil

300g (9½oz) button mushrooms,
  sliced thinly

1 clove garlic, sliced thinly

2 teaspoons thyme leaves

2 teaspoons apple cider vinegar

10g (½oz) butter

¼ cup (60g) labne (see Lorna's Tip)

1 tablespoon finely grated parmesan,
  extra

1 tablespoon finely chopped chives

1 Using a fork, whisk eggs, mylk, mustard and grated parmesan in a shallow dish until combined; season. Soak bread slices in egg mixture for 5 minutes, turning halfway through.

2 Meanwhile, heat 2 teaspoons of the oil in a large frying pan over medium-high heat; cook half the mushrooms, without stirring, for 1 minute or until browned underneath. Cook, stirring, for a further 2 minutes or until tender. Transfer to a heatproof dish; cover with foil. Repeat process with another 2 teaspoons of the oil and remaining mushrooms, adding garlic and thyme during the last minute of cooking. Stir in vinegar and half the butter. Combine mushroom mixture with mushrooms in dish; cover to keep warm.

3 In same cleaned pan, heat remaining oil and remaining butter over medium heat; cook bread for 2 minutes each side or until golden.

4 Top french toast with mushroom mixture, labne, extra grated parmesan and chopped chives. Serve with parmesan flakes and whole chives, if you like.

NUTRITIONAL COUNT PER SERVING protein (27.9g); carbohydrate (35.3g); total fat (42.5g); fibre (5.8g)

LORNA'S TIP Labne is a yoghurt cheese made by draining greek yoghurt. It's available in some supermarkets and from delis; you can leave it out or swap it for goat's cheese, if you prefer.

GREEN QUINOA WITH *Sesame Eggs*

PREP + COOK TIME 25 MINUTES SERVES 2

½ cup (100g) white quinoa, rinsed

1 cup (250g) chicken or
vegetable stock

4 free-range eggs, at room
temperature

2 teaspoons cold-pressed
extra-virgin coconut oil

1 small clove garlic, crushed

1 small red chilli, sliced

2 cups (80g) thinly sliced kale
(see Lorna's Tip)

2 cups (90g) firmly packed thinly
sliced silver beet (see Lorna's Tip)

1 tablespoon lemon juice

¼ cup finely chopped
flat-leaf parsley

1 tablespoon white sesame seeds

1 tablespoon black sesame seeds

1 teaspoon sea salt flakes

1 Place quinoa and stock in a medium saucepan;
bring to boil. Reduce heat to low-medium; simmer
gently for 15 minutes or until most of the stock
is absorbed. Remove from heat; cover and stand
for 5 minutes.

2 Meanwhile, cook eggs in a small saucepan of
boiling water for 5 minutes. Remove immediately
from pan and cool under cold running water for
30 seconds; peel shells.

3 Heat coconut oil in a medium saucepan over
medium heat. Add garlic and chilli; cook, stirring,
for 2 minutes or until fragrant. Add kale and silver
beet; stir until wilted. Stir in quinoa and juice.
Season to taste.

4 Combine parsley, sesame seeds and salt in a
small bowl. Roll peeled eggs in parsley mixture.

5 Serve green quinoa topped with halved eggs.
Sprinkle with micro red vein sorrel or extra parsley,
if you like.

NUTRITIONAL COUNT PER SERVING protein (26.9g);
carbohydrate (35.2g); total fat (26g); fibre (7.7g)

LORNA'S TIP You will need half a bunch of kale and
half a bunch of silver beet for this recipe; wash well
before use.

AVO & BROAD BEANS ON
Charcoal Brioche

PREP + COOK TIME 12 MINUTES SERVES 2

250g (8oz) frozen broad
   (fava) beans
2 tablespoons mint
2 teaspoons lemon juice
1 tablespoon cold-pressed
   extra-virgin olive oil
2 charcoal brioche burger buns
   (130g), halved
80g (2½oz) labne (see Lorna's Tip)
1 small avocado (200g), sliced thinly
1 red radish (35g), trimmed,
   sliced thinly
2 tablespoons mint leaves,
   extra, torn

1 Blanch broad beans in a saucepan of boiling salted water for 2 minutes; drain. Cool in ice-cold water; drain again. Remove and discard skins.

2 Place broad beans in a medium bowl. Add chopped mint, lemon juice and oil; season to taste.

3 Meanwhile, preheat oven grill to hot.

4 Place brioche halves under hot grill, cut-side up; cook for 2 minutes until toasted.

5 Spread brioche burger bases with labne, top with sliced avocado, broad beans, sliced radish, extra mint leaves and bun tops. Serve any leftover broad beans on the side.

NUTRITIONAL COUNT PER SERVING protein (18.2g); carbohydrate (56.9g); total fat (29.3g); fibre (11.4g)

LORNA'S TIP Labne is soft cheese made from strained yoghurt. Generally it is rolled in balls and stored in olive oil. It is available in some large supermarkets and delis. You can use soft goat's cheese, if unavailable.

SUPERFOOD *Brekkie Bowl*

PREP + COOK TIME 25 MINUTES SERVES 2

½ cup (100g) tri-coloured quinoa

1 cup (250ml) water

100g (3oz) haloumi cheese,
   sliced thickly

1 tablespoon cold-pressed
   extra-virgin olive oil

1 teaspoon dried oregano

¼ cup (40g) natural almonds,
   chopped coarsely

1 tablespoon pepitas
   (pumpkin seed kernels)

1 tablespoon sunflower seed kernels

2 teaspoons sesame seeds

1 small clove garlic, sliced

170g (5½oz) asparagus, trimmed,
   halved crossways and lengthways

100g (3oz) kale, stems removed,
   leaves torn

½ medium avocado (125g), halved

2 tablespoons sauerkraut

½ lime, cut into wedges

LEMON TAHINI DRESSING

1½ tablespoons hulled tahini

1 tablespoon lemon juice

1½ tablespoons filtered water

½ teaspoon dijon mustard

1 Rinse quinoa under running water; drain well. Place in a small saucepan with the water; bring to boil. Reduce heat; simmer, covered, for 15 minutes or until quinoa is tender.

2 Meanwhile, to make lemon tahini dressing, whisk all ingredients in a small bowl with the water until combined; season to taste.

3 Combine haloumi, 2 teaspoons of the olive oil and oregano in a bowl.

4 Toast almonds and seeds in a medium frying pan over medium heat until golden. Remove from pan.

5 Add remaining oil to frying pan. Cook garlic and asparagus over medium heat for 2 minutes or until just tender; transfer to a plate. Cook kale over medium heat for 2 minutes or until soft; add to asparagus.

6 Cook haloumi over high heat for 1 minute on each side or until golden.

7 Transfer cooked quinoa to a medium bowl. Stir in toasted almonds and seeds.

8 Serve quinoa topped with haloumi, asparagus, kale, avocado, sauerkraut and lime wedges; drizzle with lemon tahini dressing.

NUTRITIONAL COUNT PER SERVING protein (31g); carbohydrate (37.9g); total fat (53.8g); fibre (12.6g)

MIDDAY

Lunch is usually that meal where you are most tempted to buy
takeaway – you're suddenly starving, have little to no time to eat and
your next appointment is less than 30 minutes away! Sound familiar?
If so then your world is just like mine – and tends to require lunch-
on-the-go. I prepare my lunch most days, and I either make it from
scratch the night before or put it together from leftovers.

With that in mind, you'll find most of the recipes in this chapter
can be made ahead of time, happily fit into a lunch box or thermos,
and are equally delicious hot or cold, giving you plenty of midday
options for today's busy world. From tasty nutrient-packed soups to
mouth-watering superfood salads, wraps, tacos and rice paper rolls,
this chapter has plenty of super delicious, energy-packed recipes
to help you power through the second half of your day.

SPEEDY COCONUT, HERB & PEA SOUP
with Chicken

PREP + COOK TIME 20 MINUTES SERVES 4

2 tablespoons cold-pressed
  extra-virgin coconut oil
1 bunch green onions (scallions)
  (200g), sliced
1kg (2lb) frozen peas
400ml can coconut cream
3 teaspoons sea salt flakes or to taste
3 cups (750ml) boiling water
⅓ cup (80ml) lemon juice
1¾ cups coriander (cilantro) leaves
1¾ cups basil leaves
⅓ cup dill sprigs
⅓ cup mint sprigs
500g (1lb) cooked organic
  chicken breast fillets, sliced
  (see Lorna's Tips)
10g (½oz) snow pea sprouts
  (optional)
⅓ cup (95g) Greek-style yoghurt
  or unsweetened coconut yoghurt,
  to serve (optional)

1 Heat coconut oil in a large saucepan over medium-high heat. Cook onion, stirring, for 2 minutes or until softened. Increase heat to high; add peas, coconut cream, salt and the water. Bring to boil; cook, stirring occasionally, for 5 minutes or until peas are heated through.

2 Remove from heat; add lemon juice and herbs. Cool for 5 minutes. Blend or process soup, in batches, until smooth. Return soup to pan; stir until heated through. Season to taste.

3 Meanwhile, steam chicken until piping hot.

4 Serve soup in bowls. Top with chicken and snow pea sprouts; season with pepper. Serve with extra coriander and dill, yoghurt and mixed baby herbs, if you like.

NUTRITIONAL COUNT PER SERVING protein (57.6g); carbohydrate (26.3g); total fat (34g); fibre (22.1g)

LORNA'S TIPS You can poach, grill or roast the chicken breast. For a vegetarian option, leave the chicken out.

CHILLI LENTIL *Vegetable Soup*

PREP + COOK TIME 2 HOURS 45 MINUTES (+ REFRIGERATION) SERVES 4

1 tablespoon cold-pressed
extra-virgin olive oil

1 medium brown onion (150g),
chopped finely

3 cloves garlic, crushed

2 teaspoons finely grated ginger

1 teaspoon cumin seeds, crushed

1 long red chilli, chopped finely

1 medium carrot (120g),
chopped finely

2 trimmed celery stalks (200g),
chopped finely

2 fresh bay leaves

1¼ cups (185g) dried French-style
green lentils, rinsed

¼ cup (70g) no-sugar tomato paste

1½ tablespoons lemon juice

⅓ cup (25g) grated parmesan
(optional)

VEGETABLE STOCK

1 medium leek (350g)

1 large unpeeled brown onion (200g)

2 large carrots (360g)

1 large swede (400g)

2 celery stalks, with leaves (300g)

3 unpeeled cloves garlic

1 teaspoon black peppercorns

2 bay leaves

2 sprigs each rosemary, thyme
and flat-leaf parsley

5 litres (20 cups) water

1 To make vegetable stock, coarsely chop vegetables and garlic; place in a large saucepan with remaining ingredients. Bring stock to boil. Reduce heat and simmer for 2 hours. Strain stock through a sieve into a large bowl; discard solids. Leave stock to cool. Cover; refrigerate until cold.

2 Heat oil in a large saucepan over medium-high heat; cook onion, garlic, ginger, cumin, chilli, carrot and celery, stirring, for 10 minutes or until softened.

3 Add bay leaves, lentils, tomato paste and 1.5 litres (6 cups) stock; bring to boil. Reduce heat; simmer for 20 minutes or until lentils are tender. Stir in juice; season to taste.

4 Ladle soup into bowls; sprinkle with parmesan. Top with extra chilli, lemon rind and basil leaves, if you like.

NUTRITIONAL COUNT PER SERVING protein (18g); carbohydrate (27.4g); total fat (9g); fibre (10.6g)

LORNA'S TIPS Stocks are easy to prepare and will boost the flavour of any dish. The key to locking in the flavour is to cook them at a gentle simmer rather than at a boil. You can also use 1.5 litres (6 cups) of purchased vegetable stock for a short-cut. For the Eating Plan to Cleanse (pages 16–17), or for a dairy-free or vegan option, leave out the parmesan cheese.

MAKE & STASH Freeze any leftover stock in ice-cube trays for later use.

ZUCCHINI NOODLE *Beef Pho*

PREP + COOK TIME 35 MINUTES SERVES 4

1 litre (4 cups) good-quality liquid
   beef stock
2 cups (500ml) water
5cm (2in) piece ginger, sliced thinly
2 cloves garlic, sliced thinly
1 star anise
2 cinnamon sticks, broken
2 tablespoons fish sauce
½ teaspoon rapadura sugar
   (see Lorna's Tips)
4 small zucchini (360g), spiralised
   into noodles (see Lorna's Tips)
400g (12oz) piece beef fillet,
   sliced thinly
1 long red chilli, chopped finely
1 cup (80g) bean sprouts
1 cup thai basil leaves
1 cup mint leaves
1 cup coriander (cilantro) leaves
4 green onions (scallions),
   shredded
1 lime, cut into wedges

1 Place stock, the water, ginger, garlic, spices, fish sauce and sugar in a large saucepan; bring to boil. Reduce heat to low-medium; simmer for 20 minutes. Strain through a fine sieve into a large heatproof bowl; discard solids.

2 Divide zucchini noodles among bowls, then top with raw sliced beef and ladle over the hot stock. Top with chilli, bean sprouts, herbs and green onion. Serve with lime wedges.

NUTRITIONAL COUNT PER SERVING protein (45.6g); carbohydrate (5.4g); total fat (11g); fibre (3g)

LORNA'S TIPS To balance out the flavours, a little sweetener is required. I used rapadura sugar, also known as panela, which is an unrefined sugar. You can buy it from major supermarkets and health food stores. However, you can use any unrefined sugar you prefer. Spiralisers are available from kitchen and homeware stores; alternatively, you can julienne the zucchini (cut into matchsticks) using a mandoline or sharp knife.

PUMPKIN & CAULIFLOWER SOUP
with Tahini Cream

PREP + COOK TIME 1 HOUR 45 MINUTES (+ COOLING) SERVES 4

750g (1½lb) jap pumpkin, skin on,
  cut into wedges (see Lorna's Tip)
500g (1lb) parsnips, cut into rounds
¼ cup (60ml) cold-pressed
  extra-virgin olive oil
500g (1lb) cauliflower, broken into
  small florets
1 teaspoon cumin seeds
1 large brown onion (200g), chopped
1 litre (4 cups) vegetable or
  chicken stock
¼ cup (40g) pomegranate seeds
¼ cup flat-leaf parsley

TAHINI CREAM

2 tablespoons hulled tahini,
  at room temperature
¼ cup (70g) Greek-style yoghurt
1 tablespoon lemon juice
1 teaspoon water, approximately

1 Preheat oven to 200°C/400°F. Line two oven trays with baking paper.

2 Place pumpkin and parsnip on one tray; drizzle with 1 tablespoon of the oil. Season. Place cauliflower on remaining tray; drizzle with 1 tablespoon of the oil and sprinkle with cumin seeds. Season. Roast pumpkin and parsnip for 45 minutes or until soft. Remove parsnip when it is tender (it may cook faster than the pumpkin). Roast cauliflower for 40 minutes or until golden and slightly charred. Scoop the flesh from the pumpkin; discard skin.

3 Heat remaining oil in a large saucepan over medium heat; cook onion for 10 minutes or until soft. Add pumpkin flesh, parsnip and stock; bring to boil. Reduce heat; simmer, covered, for 15 minutes. Stand for 10 minutes to cool slightly.

4 Blend or process soup, in batches, until smooth. Return soup to pan over low heat; stir until hot. Season to taste.

5 Meanwhile, to make tahini cream, combine tahini, yoghurt and juice in a medium bowl. Thin down with the water, if needed.

6 Serve soup with a dollop of tahini cream and topped with cauliflower, pomegranate, parsley and a sprinkle of extra toasted cumin seeds, if you like.

NUTRITIONAL COUNT PER SERVING protein (13g); carbohydrate (36.5g); total fat (22.8g); fibre (15.1g)

LORNA'S TIP Roasting pumpkin pieces with the skin on makes a much sweeter soup.

CHILLI CHICKEN *Miso Soup*

PREP + COOK TIME 15 MINUTES SERVES 2

¼ cup (75g) dashi miso paste

3 cups (750ml) water

200g (6½oz) organic chicken breast
   fillet, sliced thinly (see Lorna's Tip)

150g (4½oz) silken tofu, cut into
   1cm cubes (or small heart shapes)

3 green onions (scallions),
   sliced thinly on the diagonal

1 long red chilli, sliced thinly
   on the diagonal

2 sheets toasted nori (seaweed),
   each cut into thin strips

2 teaspoons black sesame seeds

1 Whisk dashi miso paste and the water in a small saucepan. Bring to a simmer over medium heat. Add chicken; barely simmer for 2 minutes or until chicken is cooked.

2 Meanwhile, divide tofu, onion, chilli and nori between two bowls.

3 Pour miso soup into bowls; sprinkle with sesame seeds. Serve straight away.

NUTRITIONAL COUNT PER SERVING protein (34.5g); carbohydrate (12.8g); total fat (7.3g); fibre (2.4g)

LORNA'S TIP You could swap the chicken for sliced salmon fillet or beef rump steak.

CARROT & LENTIL SOUP
with Broccoli Pesto

PREP + COOK TIME 55 MINUTES SERVES 4

2 tablespoons cold-pressed
　　extra-virgin olive oil
1 large brown onion (200g), chopped
750g (1½lb) carrots, chopped
2 teaspoons ground cumin
2 teaspoons ground coriander
pinch dried chilli flakes
1 cup (200g) red lentils
1 litre (4 cups) vegetable stock
1½ cups (375ml) water

BROCCOLI PESTO
200g (6½oz) broccoli,
　　cut into florets
¼ cup (40g) unsalted roasted
　　cashews
⅔ cup flat-leaf parsley leaves
1 clove garlic, chopped
¼ cup (20g) finely grated parmesan
1 teaspoon finely grated lemon rind
¼ cup (60ml) lemon juice
⅓ cup (80ml) cold-pressed
　　extra-virgin olive oil

1 Heat oil in a large saucepan over medium heat; cook onion and carrot, covered, stirring occasionally, for 10 minutes or until softened. Add cumin, coriander and chilli; stir to coat. Add lentils and the stock; bring to boil. Reduce heat; simmer, covered, for 25 minutes or until lentils and carrots are soft. Cool for 5 minutes.

2 Meanwhile, to make broccoli pesto, process all ingredients except oil until finely chopped. With motor operating, add oil in a thin, steady stream. Season to taste.

3 Blend or process soup, in batches, until smooth. Return soup to pan with the water; stir over medium heat until hot. Season to taste. Serve soup topped with pesto, micro coriander and chilli oil, if you like.

NUTRITIONAL COUNT PER SERVING protein (22.7g); carbohydrate (36.7g); total fat (36.6g); fibre (18.4g)

MAKE & STASH The soup and the pesto can be made up to 3 days ahead. Cover the soup and place the pesto in an airtight container; keep both in the fridge. Soup and pesto will freeze for up to 3 months.

EAT THE RAINBOW BOWL WITH
Cashew Lemon Dressing

PREP + COOK TIME 25 MINUTES (+ STANDING) SERVES 2

125g (4oz) buckwheat soba noodles

1 teaspoon sesame oil

100g (3oz) sugar snap peas

2 red or green witlof (250g)

200g (6½oz) crunchy combo
  sprout mix

1 small avocado (200g), quartered

2 medium carrots (240g), cut into
  long matchsticks

120g (4oz) red cabbage, shredded

4 radishes (140g), trimmed,
  sliced thinly

60g (2oz) seaweed salad
  (see Lorna's Tip)

½ cup (20g) snow pea sprouts

CASHEW LEMON DRESSING

½ cup (75g) raw cashews

1 small clove garlic, crushed

¼ cup (60ml) lemon juice

2 teaspoons cold-pressed
  extra-virgin olive oil

1 To make cashew lemon dressing, place cashews in a small heatproof bowl; cover with boiling water; stand for 30 minutes. Rinse cashews; drain well. Blend cashews and the remaining ingredients until smooth.

2 Meanwhile, bring a medium saucepan of salted water to boil; cook the noodles for 5 minutes or until just tender. Remove with tongs; keep water boiling. Cool noodles under cold running water; drain. Transfer to a medium bowl; add sesame oil.

3 Blanch peas in same pan of boiling water for 30 seconds. Drain and transfer immediately to a medium bowl of cold water; drain again.

4 Divide noodles, peas, witlof, sprout mix, avocado, carrot, cabbage, radish, seaweed salad and snow pea sprouts between two large shallow bowls. Spoon over a little of the cashew lemon dressing; serve with remaining dressing to the side.

NUTRITIONAL COUNT PER SERVING protein (32.2g); carbohydrate (55.3g); total fat (41.2g); fibre (19.5g)

LORNA'S TIP Fresh seaweed salad is available from some large supermarkets and sushi stores.

SOBA NOODLE & *Tuna Salad*

PREP + COOK TIME 10 MINUTES SERVES 6

400g (12½oz) baby cucumbers
(qukes)
2 tablespoons cold-pressed
extra-virgin olive oil
600g (1¼lb) sashimi-grade tuna
270g (8½oz) dried soba noodles
1½ cups (360g) frozen shelled
edamame (soybeans)
(see Lorna's Tip)
½ cup (125ml) sushi seasoning
2 teaspoons sesame seeds
2 tablespoons mustard cress

1 Trim ends from cucumbers; using a mandoline, V-slicer or knife, cut half the cucumbers into rounds and the other half into ribbons.

2 Heat 1 teaspoon of the olive oil in a large heavy-based frying pan over high heat. Season tuna with a little salt. Cook for 30 seconds, turning on all four sides, or until browned on the outside and rare in the middle. (If you prefer, cook the tuna for a little bit longer for medium-rare.) Cool slightly, then cut into 1cm (½in) thick slices.

3 Bring a large saucepan of salted water to the boil. Add soba noodles and edamame; cook for 3 minutes or until noodles are just tender. Drain.

4 Place noodles and edamame in a large bowl with cucumber, sushi seasoning and remaining oil; toss gently to combine.

5 Serve soba salad in bowls, topped with sliced tuna. Sprinkle with sesame seeds and cress.

NUTRITIONAL COUNT PER SERVING protein (34.8g); carbohydrate (23.7g); total fat (9.8g); fibre (6.2g)

LORNA'S TIP Edamame are shelled soybeans that are usually bought frozen. They are available from Asian food stores and major supermarkets.

CRUNCHY SPROUT SALAD
with Soft-boiled Eggs

PREP + COOK TIME 20 MINUTES SERVES 2

4 free-range eggs, at room
  temperature
¾ cup (45g) firmly packed baby
  leaves (see Lorna's Tips)
100g (3oz) brussels sprouts,
  shaved thinly
1 cup (150g) crunchy combo
  sprout mix
1 small carrot (80g), sliced thinly
2 tablespoons sunflower seed kernels,
  toasted
2 tablespoons apple cider vinegar
1½ tablespoons avocado oil
1 teaspoon pure maple syrup
½ medium avocado (125g),
  sliced thinly

GREEN TAHINI DRESSING

2 tablespoons tahini
1 tablespoon lemon juice
1 cup loosely packed basil leaves
1 clove garlic, crushed

1 To make green tahini dressing, blend or process
all ingredients in a small processor until combined.
Season to taste. If the dressing is too thick, add
1–2 tablespoons water.

2 To soft boil eggs, place in a small saucepan
with enough cold water to just cover. Stir the eggs
over high heat until the water boils. Boil eggs for
3 minutes for a runny yolk or 4 minutes for an
almost-set yolk. Drain. Place under cold running
water until cool enough to handle; peel shells.

3 Place baby leaves, brussels sprouts, sprout mix,
carrot and sunflower seeds in a medium bowl; toss
to combine. Whisk vinegar, 1 tablespoon of the oil
and maple syrup in a small bowl; season to taste.
Add dressing to salad; toss to combine.

4 Divide salad between serving bowls; top with
halved eggs and avocado. Spoon green tahini dressing
over salad; drizzle with remaining oil. Season; scatter
with extra basil leaves, if you like.

NUTRITIONAL COUNT PER SERVING protein (31.1g);
carbohydrate (22.5g); total fat (47.4g); fibre (11g)

LORNA'S TIPS You can use a mixture of baby kale,
baby spinach leaves or watercress, if you like.
To make the dressing by hand, finely chop the
basil and combine all ingredients in a bowl.

Food is your friend, so make choices that work for you and help you to look and feel amazing.

BARLEY, BEET & Tomato Tabbouleh

PREP + COOK TIME 25 MINUTES SERVES 4

½ cup (100g) pearl barley
250g (8oz) grape tomatoes, sliced
1 small red onion (100g),
   chopped finely
1 large beetroot (beet) (200g),
   peeled, cut into thin matchsticks
½ cup (50g) walnuts, roasted
1 cup flat-leaf parsley leaves,
   chopped
½ cup small mint leaves, shredded
1 teaspoon finely grated lemon rind

LEMON YOGHURT DRESSING
½ cup (140g) Greek-style yoghurt
½ teaspoon finely grated lemon rind
1 tablespoon lemon juice

1 Place barley in a medium saucepan of water; bring to boil. Reduce heat to low; simmer, partially covered, for 20 minutes until tender. Drain. Rinse under cold running water; drain well.

2 Meanwhile, to make lemon yoghurt dressing, combine ingredients in a small bowl; season to taste.

3 Place barley in a large bowl with tomato, onion, beetroot, walnuts and herbs. Drizzle with dressing. Sprinkle with rind and scatter with extra parsley and mint leaves, if you like.

NUTRITIONAL COUNT PER SERVING protein (7.8g); carbohydrate (27.5g); total fat (11.5g); fibre (7.3g)

WASABI CHICKEN WITH
Cucumber & Asparagus Salad

PREP + COOK TIME 30 MINUTES SERVES 4

100g (3oz) wasabi peas

½ cup (125ml) almond mylk

8 organic chicken tenderloins (600g)

⅔ cup (160g) frozen shelled
   edamame (soybeans), thawed

1 bunch (170g) asparagus, trimmed

60g (2oz) baby spinach leaves

1 medium lebanese cucumber (130g),
   cut into ribbons

1 medium avocado (250g), diced

1 tablespoon drained pickled ginger

½ sheet toasted nori (seaweed),
   chopped finely

JAPANESE DRESSING

1 tablespoon rice wine vinegar

2 teaspoons sesame seeds, toasted
   (see Lorna's Tip)

2 tablespoons mirin

2 teaspoons tamari

½ teaspoon wasabi paste

1 small clove garlic, crushed

1 Preheat oven to 180°C/350°F. Line an oven tray with baking paper.

2 To make japanese dressing, place ingredients in a screw-top jar; shake well. Season to taste.

3 Place wasabi peas in a resealable bag. Pound peas with a rolling pin until coarsely crushed; transfer to a medium shallow dish. Place mylk in another medium shallow dish.

4 Season chicken. Dip chicken in mylk then coat in wasabi peas. Place chicken 5cm (2in) apart on tray. Bake for 15 minutes or until cooked through.

5 Meanwhile, steam edamame and asparagus separately until tender; drain. Refresh in a bowl of iced water; drain again. Place edamame in a large bowl with asparagus, spinach, cucumber, avocado, pickled ginger and nori.

6 Thickly slice chicken and gently fold through salad; drizzle with dressing. Serve straight away.

NUTRITIONAL COUNT PER SERVING protein (46.1g); carbohydrate (22.1g); total fat (14.8g); fibre (7.6g)

LORNA'S TIP To toast sesame seeds, stir seeds in a small dry frying pan over medium heat until browned lightly; cool.

SALMON *Poke Bowl*

PREP + COOK TIME 35 MINUTES SERVES 2

½ cup (100g) medium-grain
  brown rice

1 cup (250ml) water

2 tablespoons tamari

2 tablespoons lime juice

2 teaspoons cold-pressed
  extra-virgin olive oil

1 teaspoon sesame oil

1 teaspoon finely grated ginger

1 clove garlic, crushed

pinch chilli flakes

150g (4½oz) sashimi-grade salmon,
  diced (see Lorna's Tips)

3 radishes (100g), trimmed,
  sliced thinly

½ sheet toasted nori (seaweed),
  chopped (see Lorna's Tips)

1 lebanese cucumber (130g),
  sliced thinly lengthways

½ medium avocado (125g), halved

1 teaspoon sesame seeds, toasted

½ teaspoon black sesame seeds
  (optional)

½ lime, cut into 2 wedges

1 Place rice and the water in a small saucepan over low heat. Cook, covered, for 25 minutes or until tender. Drain.

2 Meanwhile, combine tamari, juice, oils, ginger, garlic and chilli flakes in a medium bowl; reserve 1 tablespoon tamari mixture for serving. Add rice to bowl with tamari mixture; toss well. Divide rice mixture between two bowls.

3 Top each bowl of rice with salmon, radish, nori, cucumber and avocado; drizzle with reserved tamari mixture. Sprinkle with sesame seeds. Serve straight away with lime wedges.

NUTRITIONAL COUNT PER SERVING protein (29.7g); carbohydrate (45.3g); total fat (28.8g); fibre (3.8g)

LORNA'S TIPS Buy the salmon from a good seafood shop with a high turnover; it must be very fresh – use it on the day of purchase. You can swap the salmon for fresh sashimi-grade tuna, if you like. I used kitchen scissors to cut the nori.

ASIAN OMELETTE SALAD
with Wasabi Dressing

PREP + COOK TIME 30 MINUTES SERVES 4

1 large carrot (180g)

1 large zucchini (150g)

3 red radishes (100g), trimmed

1 cup (80g) bean sprouts

1 cup firmly packed mint leaves

1 cup firmly packed thai basil leaves

1 cup firmly packed perilla leaves
  (see Lorna's Tips)

4 green onions (scallions),
  sliced thinly

1 long red chilli, chopped finely

320g (10oz) poached organic
  chicken breast, shredded

½ cup (80g) mixed tamari nuts
  (see recipe on page 152)

1 lime, cut into cheeks

WASABI DRESSING

2 tablespoons tamari

1 tablespoon cold-pressed
  sesame oil

1 tablespoon rice wine vinegar

1 tablespoon mirin

2 teaspoons wasabi paste

OMELETTE NOODLES

8 free-range eggs, beaten lightly

1 tablespoon tamari

pinch ground chilli powder

1 tablespoon cold-pressed
  extra-virgin olive oil

1 To make wasabi dressing, whisk all ingredients in a small bowl until combined.

2 Cut carrot, zucchini and radishes into matchsticks using a mandoline or V-slicer. Divide vegetables, sprouts, herbs, onion and chilli among bowls.

3 To make omelette noodles, whisk eggs, tamari and chilli powder together in a large bowl. Heat a large non-stick frying pan over medium-high heat. Brush with a little of the oil. Pour ⅓ cup (80ml) of the egg mixture into the pan; quickly swirl and tilt pan to coat base with egg. Cook omelette for 2 minutes or until browned underneath. Turn and cook for a further 2 minutes. Transfer omelette to a plate lined with baking paper. Repeat to make five thin omelettes. Roll omelettes into cigar shapes and slice into 2.5cm (1in) thick rings.

4 Divide omelette noodles and chicken among plates; top with nuts and serve with lime cheeks.

NUTRITIONAL COUNT PER SERVING protein (42.4g); carbohydrate (10g); total fat (38.9g); fibre (5.4g)

LORNA'S TIPS Perilla leaves, also known as shiso leaves, belong to the mint family and are available in green and purple-red varieties from Asian grocers. You can use coriander (cilantro) leaves instead, or just leave them out. For a vegetarian option, or if you are doing the Eating Plan to Cleanse on pages 16–17, leave out the chicken breast.

TEMPEH BLT *Sandwich*

PREP + COOK TIME 30 MINUTES (+ REFRIGERATION) MAKES 4

1 small avocado (200g), chopped

1 tablespoon lemon juice

8 slices multigrain sourdough bread
   (360g), toasted or fresh

40g (1½oz) baby rocket (arugula)

1 medium carrot (120g), cut into
   matchsticks

1 medium tomato (150g), sliced

¼ cup (75g) vegan mayonnaise

½ teaspoon ground turmeric

TEMPEH 'BACON'

2 tablespoons tamari

1 tablespoon cold-pressed
   extra-virgin olive oil

1 tablespoon pure maple syrup

1 teaspoon smoked paprika

300g (9½oz) tempeh, cut into
   1cm (½in) slices (see Lorna's Tips)

BEETROOT RELISH

1 tablespoon cold-pressed
   extra-virgin olive oil

1 shallot, chopped finely

½ teaspoon ground allspice

250g (8oz) all-natural vacuum-
   packed beetroot (beets),
   grated coarsely

1 tablespoons red wine vinegar

2 teaspoons pure maple syrup

1 To make tempeh 'bacon', preheat oven to 200°C/400°F. Line an oven tray with baking paper. Combine tamari, oil, maple syrup and paprika in a medium bowl. Add tempeh and toss to coat. Place tempeh, in a single layer, on tray. Bake for 20 minutes, turning halfway through cooking, until crisp.

2 Meanwhile, to make beetroot relish, heat oil in a small saucepan over low-medium heat. Cook shallot and allspice, stirring, for 5 minutes or until softened. Add beetroot, vinegar and maple syrup; cook, stirring, for 3 minutes or until vinegar evaporates. Spread out relish in a shallow bowl; refrigerate until cooled. (Makes about ¾ cup)

3 Combine avocado and juice in a small bowl; season to taste.

4 Place 4 slices of bread on a board; top with avocado mixture, rocket, carrot, beetroot relish, tomato and tempeh 'bacon'. Spoon combined mayonnaise and turmeric over tempeh. Sandwich together with remaining slices of bread.

NUTRITIONAL COUNT PER SERVING protein (17.2g); carbohydrate (54.1g); total fat (34.1g); fibre (10.7g)

LORNA'S TIPS You can swap out the tempeh for 2 small chicken breast fillets. For a short-cut, use grated raw beetroot instead of the beetroot relish.

MAKE & STASH The tempeh 'bacon' can be made up to 3 days ahead. Store any leftover relish, covered, in the fridge for up to 2 weeks.

EDAMAME FALAFEL *Wraps*

PREP + COOK TIME 30 MINUTES SERVES 4

½ cup (60g) frozen broad beans,
  skins removed
½ cup (100g) frozen shelled
  edamame (soybeans), thawed
  (see Lorna's Tips)
½ cup coriander (cilantro) leaves
1 cup (30g) baby spinach leaves
⅓ cup (45g) plain (all-purpose)
  spelt flour
½ teaspoon baking powder
1 teaspoon finely grated lemon rind
1 free-range egg
pinch pink himalayan salt
2 tablespoons sesame seeds
2 tablespoons cold-pressed
  extra-virgin olive oil
4 sweet potato wraps
  (see Lorna's Tips)
2 baby cucumbers (qukes) (80g),
  peeled lengthways into ribbons
50g (1½oz) rocket (arugula)
½ cup coriander (cilantro) sprigs,
  extra
½ cup (140g) Greek-style yoghurt
1 clove garlic, crushed
½ teaspoon ground sumac
  (optional)
black charcoal salt or himalayan
  salt, to serve (optional)

1 Preheat oven to 180°C/350°F. Line an oven tray with baking paper.

2 Place broad beans, edamame, coriander, spinach, flour, baking powder, rind, egg and salt in a food processor; process until smooth.

3 Scoop 2-tablespoonfuls of mixture onto tray and sprinkle with sesame seeds. Shape into rounds with wet hands. Drizzle with oil. Bake for 12 minutes or until golden.

4 Serve falafel in wraps with cucumber, rocket, extra coriander and combined yoghurt and garlic; sprinkle with sumac. Season with salt. Serve with chopped chillies in oil, if you like.

NUTRITIONAL COUNT PER SERVING protein (11.7g); carbohydrate (33.8g); total fat (18g); fibre (6.6g)

LORNA'S TIPS Edamame are shelled soybeans that are usually bought frozen. They are available from Asian food stores and major supermarkets. Sweet potato wraps are available from some larger supermarkets; swap for your favourite wrap if they aren't available.

PRAWN TACOS WITH
Cauliflower Tortillas

PREP + COOK TIME 30 MINUTES SERVES 4

800g (1½lb) cooked king prawns,
    peeled, deveined
1 medium avocado (250g), chopped
    (see Lorna's Tip)
4 small red radishes (60g),
    cut into matchsticks
1 small red onion (100g),
    sliced thinly
200g (6½oz) grape tomatoes, halved
1 cup coriander (cilantro) leaves
1 lime, cut into wedges
1 long red chilli, seeded, chopped
    (optional)
1½ tablespoons hot chilli sauce
    (optional)

CAULIFLOWER TORTILLAS
1.5kg (3lb) chopped cauliflower
3 free-range eggs, beaten lightly
extra-virgin olive-oil cooking spray

1 Preheat oven to 200°C/400°F.

2 To make cauliflower tortillas, process cauliflower using pulse button until pieces are finely chopped. Steam cauliflower, in two batches, for 3 minutes or until tender. Stand until cool enough to handle. Place cauliflower in a clean tea towel; squeeze out as much water as possible (this is important for dry tortillas).

3 Transfer cauliflower to a large bowl. Stir in egg; season. Divide mixture into 12 equal portions. Line three large oven trays with baking paper. Mark four 13cm (5¼in) rounds on each sheet of paper. Turn paper over; lightly spray paper with oil. Spread the cauliflower portions in rounds on trays; bake for 8 minutes. Carefully turn tortillas over using a spatula or egg slice; bake for a further 8 minutes or until browned around the edges. Cook totillas in two batches if you don't have space in the oven.

4 Serve prawns in cauliflower tortillas with avocado, radish, onion, tomato and coriander. Serve with lime wedges, chilli and chilli sauce, if you like.

NUTRITIONAL COUNT PER SERVING protein (36.2g); carbohydrate (12.3g); total fat (16.8g); fibre (13.5g)

LORNA'S TIP Sometimes I mash the avocado with a little salt and pepper and spread it thinly over each tortilla before placing the other ingredients on top.

FRAGRANT CHICKEN *Lettuce Cups*

PREP + COOK TIME 30 MINUTES SERVES 4

1 tablespoon jasmine rice

1 tablespoon cold-pressed
    extra-virgin coconut oil

3 cloves garlic, chopped

1 lemon grass stalk, white part only,
    sliced thinly

3 kaffir lime leaves, shredded

500g (1lb) organic minced
    (ground) chicken

1 small fennel (130g), sliced thinly

8 baby cos (romaine) lettuce leaves

1 long green chilli, sliced thinly

½ cup small mint leaves

1 lime, cut into wedges

VIETNAMESE DRESSING

¼ cup (60ml) fish sauce

¼ cup (60ml) lime juice

½ teaspoon liquid stevia

1   To make vietnamese dressing, whisk ingredients until well combined.

2   Cook rice in a small frying pan over medium-high heat, stirring, for 3 minutes or until lightly toasted. Pound toasted rice in a mortar and pestle until coarsely crushed.

3   Heat oil in a large non-stick frying pan over medium heat. Add garlic, lemon grass and two-thirds of the lime leaves; cook, stirring, for 30 seconds or until fragrant.

4   Increase heat to high. Add chicken to pan; cook, stirring to break up lumps, for 7 minutes or until cooked. Add half the dressing; cook, stirring, for 1 minute.

5   Spoon chicken mixture and fennel into lettuce leaves; top with half the chilli, remaining lime leaves, the mint and crushed rice. Add remaining chilli to remaining dressing. Serve dressing with lettuce cups and lime wedges.

NUTRITIONAL COUNT PER SERVING protein (26.4g); carbohydrate (5.9g); total fat (15g); fibre (1.9g)

LORNA'S TIP If I'm taking leftovers for lunch, I simply shred the lettuce and layer the chicken mix on top. This makes it easier to eat at my desk.

PEA, MINT & MISO *Rice Paper Rolls*

PREP + COOK TIME 30 MINUTES MAKES 10 ROLLS

2 cups (240g) frozen peas, thawed

1 tablespoon white (shiro) miso paste

1 teaspoon finely grated lime rind

1 tablespoon lime juice

¼ cup coarsely chopped mint leaves

10 x 22cm (9in) rice papers rounds

1 large avocado (320g), sliced thinly

2 cups (160g) finely shredded
   purple cabbage

½ small daikon (200g), cut into
   matchsticks

10 mint leaves

¼ cup mustard cress (optional)

1 teaspoon black sesame seeds

**SESAME GINGER DIPPING
   SAUCE**

70g (2½oz) piece ginger,
   grated finely

¼ cup (70g) unhulled tahini

2 tablespoons sesame oil

2 tablespoons tamari

2 tablespoons apple cider vinegar

2 tablespoons yacon syrup or
   coconut nectar (see Lorna's Tips)

½ long red chilli, seeded,
   sliced thinly (optional)

1 To make dipping sauce, press grated ginger through a sieve over a small bowl; you will need 2 tablespoons of ginger juice. Discard pulp. Combine ginger juice with tahini, sesame oil, tamari, vinegar and yacon syrup in a small bowl; stir until smooth. Add chilli, if you like.

2 Mash peas lightly in a medium bowl with miso, rind, juice and mint until combined; season to taste.

3 Place 1 rice paper round in a medium bowl of lukewarm water for 15 seconds or until just soft. Place on a clean tea towel or paper towel.

4 Place one-tenth of the avocado slices, cabbage and daikon in the centre of the rice paper round; top with one-tenth of the pea mixture, mint and cress. Fold edges in and roll up firmly to enclose filling. Repeat with remaining rice paper rounds and filling ingredients to make ten rolls. Sprinkle rolls and dipping sauce with sesame seeds; serve.

NUTRITIONAL COUNT PER ROLL protein (4.7g); carbohydrate (11.1g); total fat (12.8g); fibre (4.6g)

LORNA'S TIPS Yacon syrup is available from some health food stores. It has a consistency similar to rice malt syrup, with a distinctive treacle-like flavour and a mild level of sweetness. Rolls are best made on the day of serving; make a few hours ahead, then store, covered with damp paper towel, in an airtight container in the fridge.

MAKE & STASH Dipping sauce will keep for up to 1 week; store in a sealed glass jar in the fridge.

SUPERCHARGED SNACKS

Having a few supercharged nutritious snacks between meals is a wonderful way to keep your energy levels high, your metabolism going and, in my opinion, absolutely essential to ward off any mid-morning or mid-afternoon junk food cravings. Snacks are an integral part of my daily food plan, and I understand that it's important to have them on-hand but also know that it's equally important not to reach for them just because they're there.
The recipes in this section are some of my all-time favourites and you'll find that there is a good mix of savoury and sweet, with some that can be made ahead of time and stored in the fridge or freezer and others that are quick and easy to make on the go.

AVOCADO BOATS WITH
Miso Sauce & Cashews

PREP + COOK TIME 15 MINUTES SERVES 4

1½ tablespoons white (shiro) miso paste

2 tablespoons almond butter

2 tablespoons cold-pressed extra-virgin olive oil

½ teaspoon sesame oil

1 tablespoon mirin

1 tablespoon water

2 small avocados (400g)

⅓ cup (50g) roasted cashews, chopped coarsely

½ teaspoon black sesame seeds

1 Stir miso, almond butter, oils, mirin and the water in a medium jug until smooth; season to taste.

2 Cut unpeeled avocados in half; discard stones. Cut diagonal lines in avocados to form diamonds, without cutting through to the the skin. Spoon miso mixture into avocado hollows; sprinkle with cashews and sesame seeds. Serve straight away.

NUTRITIONAL COUNT PER SERVING protein (6.7g); carbohydrate (6.8g); total fat (36.2g); fibre (4.2g)

LORNA'S TIPS You could also quarter the avocados for smaller appetites. The miso mixture can also be used as a dressing for salads. Use any of your favourite healthy dressings or dips for this quick and easy snack.

MAKE & STASH Miso mixture will keep in an airtight container in the fridge for up to 2 weeks.

CHAI-SPICED *Popcorn*

PREP + COOK TIME 8 MINUTES SERVES 4

2 tablespoons cold-pressed
  extra-virgin olive oil
  (see Lorna's Tips)
1 tablespoon powdered stevia
  or norbu (monk fruit sugar)
2 teaspoons ground cinnamon
1 teaspoon ground ginger
½ teaspoon ground cardamom
½ teaspoon ground allspice
½ teaspoon sea salt flakes
1 tablespoon cold-pressed
  extra-virgin olive oil, extra
½ cup (120g) popping corn

1 Combine oil, stevia, spices and salt in a small bowl.

2 Heat the extra oil in a large saucepan over
medium heat. Add popping corn and cover pan;
cook, shaking the pan occasionally, for 2 minutes
or until popping stops.

3 Place popcorn in a large bowl. Drizzle with spice
mixture; stir until well coated.

NUTRITIONAL COUNT PER SERVING protein (4g);
carbohydrate (17.3g); total fat (15g); fibre (5g)

LORNA'S TIPS Use a mild flavoured olive oil for this
recipe. If you have one, it's handy to use a saucepan
with a glass lid so you can see if all the corn has
popped. Popcorn can be made a day ahead; cool and
store in an airtight container.

TOASTED NORI *Chips*

PREP + COOK TIME 15 MINUTES MAKES 60

2 teaspoons sesame seeds

1 teaspoon sea salt, crumbled

10 sheets nori (seaweed)

2 tablespoons sesame oil

JAPANESE SPRINKLE

1 tablespoon finely grated
    orange rind

2 teaspoons cracked black pepper

1 tablespoon chilli flakes

2 teaspoons black sesame seeds

1 To make japanese sprinkle, dry-fry rind in a large frying pan over medium heat for 5 minutes or until rind is dry and crispy. Place in a screw-top jar with pepper, chilli and black sesame seeds; shake well to combine.

2 Crush sesame seeds using a mortar and pestle; combine with 2 teaspoons of the japanese sprinkle and the salt. (Store remaining japanese sprinkle for another use.)

3 Using scissors, cut each nori sheet into strips or squares. Place on a large baking-paper-lined tray; lightly brush nori with sesame oil.

4 Heat a large non-stick frying pan over medium-high heat; toast nori, in batches, for 2 minutes each side or until crisp. Return to paper-lined tray; scatter with japanese sprinkle.

NUTRITIONAL COUNT PER CHIP protein (0.2g); carbohydrate (0.2g); total fat (0.8g); fibre (0.1g)

MAKE & STASH The chips will keep in an airtight container in a cool, dry place for 2 weeks.

CARROT & TURMERIC HUMMUS
with Sumac Chips

PREP + COOK TIME 12 MINUTES MAKES 3 CUPS SERVES 8

2 x 400g (12½oz) cans chickpeas
   (garbanzo beans)
1 clove garlic, crushed
¼ cup (70g) tahini
¼ cup (60ml) lemon juice
¼ cup (60ml) cold-pressed
   extra-virgin olive oil
1½ cups (360g) coarsely grated
   carrot
¾ teaspoon ground turmeric

SUMAC CHIPS
4 pieces mountain bread (100g)
2 tablespoons cold-pressed
   extra-virgin olive oil
2 teaspoons ground sumac

1 To make sumac chips, preheat oven to 180°C/350°F. Place bread on oven trays. Brush with oil and sprinkle with sumac. Bake for 5 minutes or until crisp. Cool; break into pieces.

2 Meanwhile, drain chickpeas, reserving ½ cup liquid. Place chickpeas, garlic, tahini, juice and oil in a food processer and process until smooth.

3 Add carrot and turmeric; process until smooth. If mixture is too thick, gradually add some of the reserved liquid until the correct consistency. Season.

4 Sprinkle hummus with a little extra sumac. Serve with sumac chips.

NUTRITIONAL COUNT PER SERVING protein (7.2g); carbohydrate (18.7g); total fat (18.4g); fibre (6.2g)

MAKE & STASH Keep hummus in the fridge and chips in a container in a dry place for up to 1 week.

GREEN HUMMUS Make hummus in step 2. In step 3, omit the carrot and turmeric and instead add ½ cup each coriander (cilantro) leaves and mint leaves; process hummus mixture until smooth. Serve topped with 60g (2oz) crumbled fetta. Drizzle with a little extra olive oil.

SEED & SPICE HUMMUS Make hummus in step 2. In step 3, omit carrot and turmeric. Heat 2 tablespoons olive oil in a small frying pan over medium heat; cook 2 tablespoons pepitas (pumpkin seed kernels) and 1 teaspoon each cumin and sesame seeds, stirring, for 3 minutes or until toasted. Drizzle hummus with extra oil and sprinkle with spice mixture.

LORNA'S TIP I usually make two of the hummus recipes so I have a little variety throughout the week. I swap between eating them with the sumac chips and freshly chopped vegetables such as cucumbers and carrots.

1

2

PICK-YOUR-
FLAVOUR

Yoghurt

3

4

LORNA'S TIP These are the
most delicious yoghurts ever!
I make one every week and
use it as a replacement for
cream and ice-cream.

COCONUT YOGHURT

PREP TIME 10 MINUTES MAKES 3 CUPS

Cut open 2 drinking coconuts and pour coconut
water into a bowl. Scrape flesh out of coconuts
and place in a high-powered blender with 1 cup
(150g) raw cashews, ½ cup (125ml) filtered water,
1 tablespoon pure maple syrup, 1 teaspoon
vanilla bean paste, a pinch himalayan salt,
1 probiotic capsule (optional) and 1 cup of
the coconut water. Blend until smooth.

Flavour variations

GINGER & PEACH

Stir 1 tablespoon finely grated ginger into
yoghurt along with 2 chopped ripe peaches
and ⅓ cup toasted flaked coconut.

NUTTY CHERRY SWIRL

Combine ⅓ cup tahini with 2 tablespoons pure
maple syrup in a bowl. Stir in 12 seeded and
chopped cherries and ¼ cup chopped walnuts.
Layer or swirl with yoghurt.

BASIL STRAWBERRIES

Hull 125g (4oz) strawberries and halve. Place in
a bowl and mash with a fork. Stir in 2 tablespoons
shredded basil. Swirl through yoghurt. Decorate
with basil sprigs, if you like.

MANGO & MACADAMIA

Cut cheeks from 1 mango and scoop out flesh.
Mash in a bowl with the juice of 1 lime until
pulpy. Stir in ¼ cup chopped macadamias.
Fold through yoghurt. Top with 2 chopped
green kiwifruit. Serve with extra sliced mango
and extra chopped macadamias, if you like.

BANANA, CHOC &
Peanut Butter Wraps

PREP TIME 5 MINUTES SERVES 2

4 rainbow chard leaves, rinsed and
   dried (see Lorna's Tips)
2 tablespoons crunchy peanut butter
   (see Lorna's Tips)
2 medium ripe bananas (400g),
   cut in half crossways
1 tablespoon pure maple syrup
2 tablespoons coarsely chopped
   dark chocolate (70% cocoa)
½ teaspoon ground cinnamon

1 Remove stalks and trim centre vein from rainbow chard (reserve stalks for another use; see Lorna's Tips).

2 Place the leaves, stalk-sides down, and spread peanut butter along centres. Place banana halves crossways across middle of leaves. Drizzle with maple syrup; sprinkle with chocolate and cinnamon.

3 Fold in the sides and roll up firmly to enclose the filling (like a rice paper roll). Secure with a toothpick and cut in half with a serrated knife.

NUTRITIONAL COUNT PER SERVING protein (10.2g); carbohydrate (37.1g); total fat (17.4g); fibre (6g)

LORNA'S TIPS Rainbow chard is similar to silver beet but with colourful stalks. Use the smaller, younger leaves as they are easier to roll. If you have difficulty rolling them, place the leaves in a large bowl and pour over boiling water; stand for 10 seconds to just soften, then drain well and dry with paper towel. You can use the reserved stalks in your next stir-fry. Try swapping the peanut butter for my Nut & Seed Butter on page 146.

This is the perfect afternoon snack to have before a workout.

PEANUT BUTTER & MISO DIP
with Cinnamon Crackers

PREP TIME 10 MINUTES SERVES 6

2 tablespoons white (shiro)
  miso paste
½ cup (145g) natural crunchy
  peanut butter
2 tablespoons sesame oil
1½ tablespoons rice wine vinegar
3 teaspoons mirin
¼ cup (60ml) cold water
2 teaspoons sesame seeds, toasted
vegetable crudites, to serve
  (optional)

CINNAMON CRACKERS
2 large wholemeal lebanese bread
  (190g)
1 tablespoon cold-pressed
  extra-virgin olive oil
1 teaspoon ground cinnamon
  (see Lorna's Tips)

1 To make cinnamon crackers, preheat oven to 180°C/350°F. Split bread in half horizontally to make 4 thin pieces; place on oven trays. Brush with oil and sprinkle with cinnamon. Bake for 5 minutes or until crisp. Cool; break into pieces.

2 Combine miso, peanut butter, oil, vinegar, mirin and the water in a medium bowl.

3 Transfer dip to a clean bowl; sprinkle with sesame seeds. Serve with cinnamon crackers and crudites, if you like.

NUTRITIONAL COUNT PER SERVING (WITHOUT CRUDITES)
protein (12.1g); carbohydrate (24.7g); total fat (27.3g); fibre (4.9g)

LORNA'S TIPS If you have the time, I find that buying cinnamon sticks and grinding them yourself makes for a more fragrant and delicious ground cinnamon – for this recipe and just about everything else that requires this spice. This dip is great to take out and about for snacking, as it does not require refrigeration. The dip will firm if refrigerated, so bring it to room temperature before serving.

SWEET POTATO *Energy Balls*

PREP + COOK TIME 1 HOUR (+ STANDING) MAKES 30

1½ cups (225g) raw cashews

800g (1½lb) orange sweet potatoes, cut into 2cm (¾in) pieces

⅓ cup (80ml) cold-pressed extra-virgin olive oil

1 tablespoon cumin seeds, toasted, crushed

¼ cup (50g) pepitas (pumpkin seed kernels), chopped coarsely

45g (1½oz) dukkah

1 sheet toasted nori (seaweed), chopped finely

1 tablespoon psyllium husks

1 tablespoon almond meal

green salad and hummus or Greek-style yoghurt, to serve (see Lorna's Tip)

1 Soak cashews in a heatproof bowl of boiling water for 30 minutes; drain well.

2 Meanwhile, preheat oven to 180°C/350°F. Line two large oven trays with baking paper.

3 Toss sweet potato, 2 tablespoons of the oil and cumin together; season with salt. Transfer to one of the trays; roast for 25 minutes or until almost tender. Add cashews; roast for a further 12 minutes or until sweet potato is tender and cashews are golden.

4 Heat pepitas in a large heavy-based frying pan over medium heat, stirring, for 4 minutes or until toasted lightly. Add dukkah and nori; cook, stirring frequently, for 2 minutes or until fragrant. Transfer to second lined tray.

5 Process sweet potato, cashews, psyllium and almond meal until combined coarsely; season to taste. Using wet hands, roll level tablespoonfuls of warm mixture into balls; coat in dukkah mixture.

6 Heat remaining oil in a non-stick frying pan over medium heat. Cook balls for 3 minutes, turning, or until golden brown all over. Top with micro red vein sorrel, if you like; serve with a green salad and hummus or Greek-style yoghurt.

NUTRITIONAL COUNT PER BALL protein (2.8g); carbohydrate (7g); total fat (7.9g); fibre (1.3g)

LORNA'S TIPS These are a great snack served hot or cold (I usually have three). They are also great for lunch – serve them with a big green salad, such as the Cucumber & Asparagus Salad on page 102 or the Crunchy Sprout Salad on page 96. For a more substantial snack, serve them with one of the hummus recipes on pages 127 or 159.

The best diet in the world is one that is varied
– so be sure to eat as many different real foods as possible.

COCONUT, PECAN & APRICOT Bar

PREP TIME 25 MINUTES (+ REFRIGERATION) MAKES 24

1 cup (120g) almond meal

1 cup (80g) desiccated coconut

⅓ cup (55g) white chia seeds

1 cup (240g) cold-pressed
   extra-virgin coconut oil, melted
   (see Lorna's Tips)

⅓ cup (80ml) pure maple syrup

1 cup (90g) rolled oats

1 cup (150g) sunflower seed kernels

1 cup (200g) pepitas
   (pumpkin seed kernels)

1 cup (120g) pecans, chopped finely
   (see Lorna's Tips)

½ cup (75g) sulphite-free
   dried apricots, chopped finely
   (see Lorna's Tips)

8 fresh dates (160g), pitted,
   chopped finely (see Lorna's Tips)

1 Grease a 20cm x 30cm (8in x 12in) slice pan with a little coconut oil; line base and sides with baking paper, extending the paper 5cm (2in) over the edges.

2 Combine almond meal, desiccated coconut and chia seeds in a medium bowl. Add half the oil and ¼ cup of the maple syrup; mix well to combine. Press the almond mixture into the pan; level the top.

3 Combine oats, seeds, pecans, apricots and dates in a medium bowl. Add the remaining coconut oil and maple syrup; mix well to combine. Place fruit mixture over almond mixture and press down very firmly. Cover; refrigerate for 4 hours or until chilled and firm. Cut into 24 bars.

NUTRITIONAL COUNT PER BAR protein (6.3g); carbohydrate (12.9g); total fat (26.9g); fibre (4.3g)

LORNA'S TIPS Coconut oil is a solidified oil sold in jars and is available from major supermarkets and health food stores. Melt coconut oil as you would butter, in a small saucepan over low heat. It is important to finely chop the pecans, apricots and dates to ensure that the topping ingredients hold together. Or, if preferred, you can pulse them in a food processor until finely chopped.

MAKE & STASH Bars will keep, covered, in an airtight container in the fridge for up to 1 month, or freeze them for up to 3 months.

SWEET & SOUR ROASTED
Chickpea & Bean Mix

PREP + COOK TIME 1 HOUR   MAKES 2½ CUPS   SERVES 8

2 x 400g (12½oz) cans chickpeas
   (garbanzo beans)
2 x 400g (12½oz) cans butter beans
1 tablespoon cold-pressed
   extra-virgin olive oil
1 tablespoon finely grated lime rind
2 teaspoons ground cumin
2 teaspoons ground coriander
1 teaspoon chilli flakes
1 tablespoon coconut sugar

1   Preheat oven to 220°C/425°F. Line an oven tray with baking paper.

2   Drain and rinse chickpeas and beans. Place in a medium heatproof bowl. Cover with boiling water; stand for 1 minute, then drain. Pat dry on paper towel or a clean tea towel (this is to ensure the chickpeas and beans will dry and crisp during roasting).

3   Place chickpeas and beans on tray. Bake for 50 minutes, stirring occasionally, or until chickpeas and beans are golden and crisp.

4   Transfer roasted chickpeas and beans to a medium bowl. Add combined oil, rind, cumin, coriander, chilli flakes and coconut sugar. Season generously with salt and freshly ground black pepper; toss until well coated.

NUTRITIONAL COUNT PER SERVING   protein (5.4g); carbohydrate (13.1g); total fat (3.9g); fibre (4.5g)

LORNA'S TIPS   You can use dried chickpeas and dried butter or lima beans instead of the canned chickpeas and butter beans. Soak them overnight first, then cook for 1½ hours in boiling water. Experiment with different spices and herbs to flavour them however you like.

MAKE & STASH   Store the roasted mix in an airtight container or jar for up to 4 days.

GREEN GODDESS Mini Frittatas

PREP + COOK TIME 35 MINUTES MAKES 8

2 teaspoons cold-pressed
  extra-virgin olive oil
1 long green chilli, seeded, chopped
  coarsely (optional)
4 green onions (scallions), chopped
3 cups (120g) firmly packed baby
  kale or baby spinach leaves,
  chopped
1 tablespoon chopped mint
1 tablespoon chopped basil
1 tablespoon chopped flat-leaf parsley
½ cup (125ml) almond mylk or
  rice mylk
5 free-range eggs
pinch pink himalayan salt
80g (2½oz) goat's cheese

1 Preheat oven to 180°C/350°F. Line 8 holes of a
12-hole (⅓-cup/80ml) muffin pan with paper cases.

2 Heat oil in a medium frying pan over medium
heat; cook chilli and onion, stirring, for 3 minutes
or until onion is soft.

3 Meanwhile, blend 1 cup of the kale with the herbs
and almond mylk until smooth.

4 Whisk eggs and kale puree in a medium jug until
combined; season with the salt.

5 Divide chopped kale and onion mixture among
pan holes; pour over egg mixture. Top with crumbled
goat's cheese.

6 Bake frittatas for 20 minutes or until set;
they will become firmer on standing. Leave in
pan for 5 minutes before serving warm or at room
temperature. Scatter with extra fresh herbs,
if you like.

NUTRITIONAL COUNT PER FRITTATA protein (7g);
carbohydrate (0.9g); total fat (6.6g); fibre (0.6g)

MAKE & STASH Store frittatas in an airtight container
in the fridge for up to 5 days.

SERVING SUGGESTIONS I eat two as a snack or three
with roast vegetables or a big green salad for lunch.

SENSATIONAL *Seed Crackers*

PREP + COOK TIME 1 HOUR 30 MINUTES (+ COOLING) MAKES 50

1 cup (200g) long-grain brown rice
2½ cups (625ml) water
1 cup (200g) tri-colour quinoa
2 cups (500ml) water, extra
¼ cup (40g) sesame seeds
¼ cup (50g) linseeds (flaxseeds)
¼ cup (35g) chia seeds
¼ cup (35g) sunflower seed kernels
2 tablespoons finely chopped oregano
1 tablespoon onion powder
1 teaspoon cracked black pepper

1 Place brown rice and the water in a small saucepan; bring to boil. Reduce heat to low; simmer, uncovered, for 25 minutes or until most of the water evaporates. Remove from heat; stand, covered, for 10 minutes. Fluff with a fork. Spread out over an oven tray; cool.

2 Meanwhile, place quinoa and the extra water in same pan; bring to boil. Reduce heat to low; simmer, uncovered, for 10 minutes or until most of the water evaporates. Remove from heat; stand, covered, for 10 minutes. Fluff with a fork. Spread out over an oven tray; cool.

3 Preheat oven to 180°C/350°F.

4 Process the rice with half the quinoa to a coarse paste; transfer to a large bowl. Add remaining quinoa and remaining ingredients; season. Using your hands, combine well. Divide into four portions.

5 Line four oven trays with baking paper. Remove one of the pieces of paper. Flatten a portion of dough on the paper; cover with plastic wrap, then roll out with a rolling pin to 1mm (¹⁄₁₆in) thick or as thin as possible (don't worry if there are holes; these will give the crackers texture and character). Discard plastic; carefully lift the paper back onto the tray. Repeat with remaining portions of dough. Score the crackers into 5cm x 10cm (2in x 4in) lengths or triangles (or leave as whole sheets and break into pieces after baking).

6 Bake crackers for 20 minutes. Cover crackers with a sheet of baking paper and a second tray. Holding the hot tray with oven gloves, flip the crackers over onto the second tray. Carefully remove lining paper. Repeat with remaining trays of crackers. Cook crackers for a further 20 minutes until golden and crisp. Cool on trays.

NUTRITIONAL COUNT PER CRACKER protein (1.5g); carbohydrate (5.7g); total fat (1.8g); fibre (1g)

LORNA'S TIPS If the cracker mixture spreads past the paper when you're rolling it, just cut those edges off. If you don't have enough oven trays, you can cook the crackers in two batches.

MAKE & STASH Crackers can be stored in an airtight container for up to 1 month.

SERVING SUGGESTIONS Serve crackers with labne or avocado mashed with chilli flakes and chopped coriander (cilantro).

NUT & SEED *Butter*

PREP TIME 15 MINUTES (+ REFRIGERATION) MAKES 1½ CUPS

1 cup (160g) blanched almonds,
  roasted
½ cup (70g) roasted unsalted
  peanuts
½ cup (75g) sunflower seed kernels
¼ cup (40g) linseeds (flaxseeds)
¼ cup (60ml) cold-pressed
  extra-virgin olive oil
1 tablespoon pure maple syrup
½ teaspoon sea salt flakes

1 Process all ingredients, scraping the side of the bowl regularly, until the mixture is smooth. If you can, use a high-powered blender for a faster and smoother result. (This step may take up to 25 minutes, depending on the processing power of your processor or blender. Powerful commercial processors and blenders will take around 10 minutes, while small home-use blenders/processors can take up to 25 minutes before the mixture becomes smooth.)

2 Spoon nut and seed butter into a jar and refrigerate. Give the butter a stir before using as the oil will settle on the top.

NUTRITIONAL COUNT PER 1 TABLESPOON protein (4.1g); carbohydrate (1.8g); total fat (12.9g); fibre (2.2g)

LORNA'S TIP For a crunchy nut butter, reserve ½ cup of the nuts and pulse through at the end of blending.

MAKE & STASH The nut butter will keep in an airtight container in the fridge for up to 3 weeks.

SERVING SUGGESTIONS Spread the nut butter on your favourite toast or crispbread, then top with thinly sliced fruit such as banana, strawberries or apple. Sliced avocado with sesame seeds works well too.

CACAO & MAPLE BUTTER For a Nutella-like spread, add 1½ tablespoons cacao powder and an extra 1 tablespoon maple syrup to the ingredients.

CASHEW & MACADAMIA BUTTER Swap the almonds and peanuts with cashews and macadamias, and omit the linseeds.

This delicious non-dairy butter alternative is suitable not only for vegans but also for those who are lactose intolerant. This butter is very lightly sweetened but can still be used as a spread for savoury sandwiches. Simply omit the maple syrup, if you prefer.

INCREDIBLE SEED *Bread*

PREP + COOK TIME 1 HOUR 15 MINUTES (+ STANDING & COOLING) MAKES 12 SLICES

⅓ cup (30g) psyllium husks

1½ cups (375ml) filtered water

1 cup (150g) sunflower seed kernels

½ cup (100g) pepitas
   (pumpkin seed kernels)

½ cup (85g) activated buckwheat
   groats (see Lorna's Tips)

½ cup (80g) linseeds (flaxseeds)

½ cup (80g) white sesame seeds

¼ cup (50g) black chia seeds

1½ teaspoons pink himalayan salt

¼ cup (60g) cold-pressed
   extra-virgin coconut oil, melted

1 tablespoon chopped rosemary

rosemary sprigs, extra (optional)

1 Preheat oven to 180°C/350°F. Grease a 10cm x 20cm (4in x 8in) loaf pan with a 1.5-litre (6-cup) capacity. Line base and sides with baking paper, extending paper 5cm (2in) over long sides.

2 Combine psyllium husks with the water in a small bowl; stand for 5 minutes or until it forms a thick gel-like paste.

3 Combine remaining ingredients, except rosemary sprigs, in a large bowl; add psyllium gel. Using hands, mix well and massage the gel through the seeds. Spoon mixture into pan; smooth top. Stand for 1 hour to absorb liquid. Scatter with extra rosemary sprigs, if you like.

4 Bake loaf for 1 hour or until firm to touch and golden. Cool in pan; turn onto a wire rack. Let the bread cool completely before slicing.

NUTRITIONAL COUNT PER SLICE protein (9.6g); carbohydrate (6.8g); total fat (23.8g); fibre (7.2g)

LORNA'S TIPS Activated buckwheat groats are available from health food stores. You can substitute with rolled oats, nuts or more seeds, if you prefer. To make a sweeter bread, add dried cranberries or dried apricots in step 3 and serve topped with labne and sliced banana.

MAKE & STASH Store bread in an airtight container in the fridge for up to 1 week, or slice and freeze for up to 2 months.

SERVING SUGGESTIONS Bread is best eaten toasted and is delicious spread with avocado.

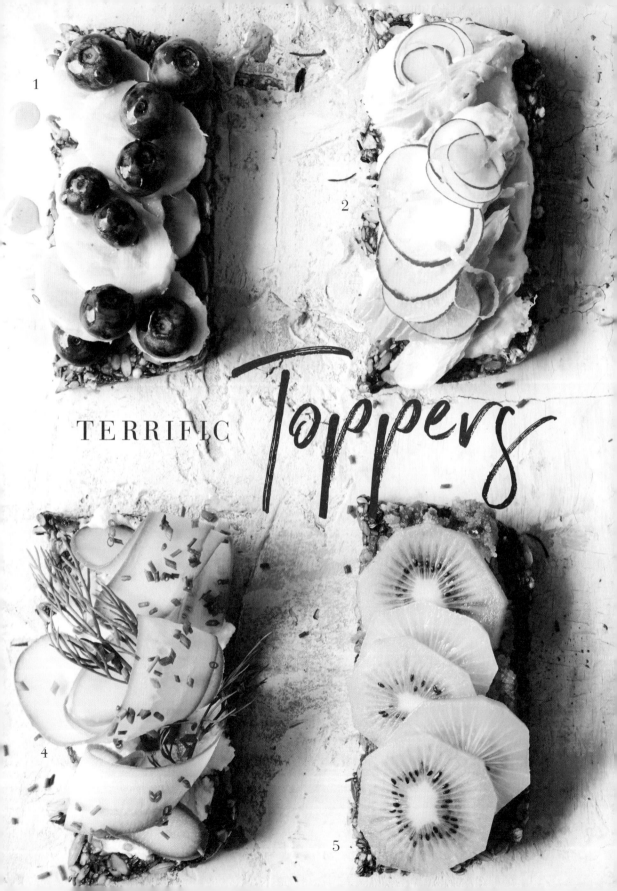

TERRIFIC *Toppers*

1

2

4

5

Use these terrific toppers on my Incredible Seed Bread on page 149 or on grilled sweet potato 'toast'.

NUTS, SEEDS & BERRIES

Spread 4 slices bread with ⅓ cup Nut & Seed Butter (see page 146). Divide 1 thinly sliced banana and ⅓ cup blueberries between slices and drizzle each with 1 teaspoon maple syrup.

LEMON & OCEAN TROUT

Spread ⅔ cup Greek-style yoghurt and 1 teaspoon grated lemon rind on 4 slices bread. Top with 200g (6½oz) flaked hot-smoked ocean trout, 4 thinly sliced radishes and lemon zest.

AVOCADO & DUKKAH

Divide 1 sliced avocado between 4 slices bread; squeeze over half a lemon. Top with 100g (3oz) crumbled goat's cheese and 1 tablespoon dukkah.

GOAT'S CHEESE & QUKES

Spread 125g (4oz) goat's cheese combined with 2 tablespoons chopped chives on 4 slices bread. Top with 2 baby cucumbers (qukes) (80g), peeled lengthways into ribbons, dill and extra chives.

CASHEW BUTTER & KIWI

Spread 4 slices bread with ⅓ cup cashew butter. Thinly slice 1 green and 1 gold kiwifruit; divide between slices.

EDAMAME & EGG

Prepare 1 cup (200g) frozen shelled edamame following packet instructions; drain, then coarsely mash. Divide between 4 slices bread. Top with 4 halved soft-boiled eggs. Sprinkle with micro cress and a pinch of ground sumac.

TOTALLY ADDICTIVE *Tamari Nut Mix*

PREP + COOK TIME 25 MINUTES (+ STANDING) MAKES 3 CUPS SERVES 12

2 tablespoons tamari

1 teaspoon finely grated lime rind

¼ teaspoon cayenne pepper

½ teaspoon pink himalayan salt

1 cup (160g) natural almonds

1 cup (150g) raw cashews

1 cup (140g) raw macadamias

1 Preheat oven to 150°C/300°F. Line two oven trays with baking paper.

2 Combine tamari, lime rind, cayenne pepper and salt in a medium bowl. Add nuts and mix well; stand for 1 hour to absorb the tamari.

3 Divide nut mixture evenly between trays.

4 Roast nuts for 20 minutes, stirring occasionally, or until dry and browned. Cool nuts on trays.

NUTRITIONAL COUNT PER SERVING protein (5.8g); carbohydrate (3.4g); total fat (22.3g); fibre (2.6g)

LORNA'S TIP I portion handfuls of the nut mix into small airtight containers and take them to work as a quick and easy mid-morning or mid-afternoon snack.

MAKE & STASH Store in an airtight container or jar for up to 1 week.

EVENINGS

Evenings are the perfect time to kick-back with good company and delicious food but also a great opportunity to balance out your nutrient intake for the day, relax and really take the time to enjoy your food. On most days, by the time I've finished work, there's a seriously short amount of time between when I get home and when I'm ready to eat – so the majority of recipes in this section are for all the busy people (like me!) who want something incredibly delicious and nutritious to eat at the end of the day but also need their evening meal to be quick and easy to make. There are also some weekend favourites for when you have a little more time. But what I do know for sure is that from main-meal-worthy salads, to mouth-watering curries, quick and easy burgers and my family's favourite lasagne – the dinner options in this section will soon be on high rotation in your kitchen – because they really do take the fuss (but none of the flavour) out of your all-important evening meal.

EASY VEGAN BURGERS
in Charcoal Buns

PREP + COOK TIME 40 MINUTES SERVES 4

400g (12½oz) can black beans,
   drained, rinsed (see Lorna's Tip)
1 medium beetroot (beet) (150g),
   grated
80g (2½oz) flat mushrooms,
   chopped finely
¼ medium red onion (45g),
   chopped finely
1 teaspoon finely grated ginger
1 medium clove garlic, crushed
2 tablespoons tamari
1½ tablespoons cold-pressed
   extra-virgin olive oil
1 teaspoon ground cumin
⅛ teaspoon ground chilli powder
½ cup (45g) rolled oats
¼ cup (35g) sunflower seed kernels
¼ cup (25g) ground golden linseeds
   (flaxseeds)
1 small carrot (80g)
1 medium beetroot (beet) (150g),
   extra
4 charcoal burger buns, halved
1 medium avocado (250g), mashed
30g (1oz) mixed salad leaves
½ cup (40g) shredded red cabbage
VEGAN CHILLI MAYO
⅓ cup (100g) vegan mayonnaise
2 teaspoons hot chilli sauce

1 Preheat oven to 220°C/425°F.

2 Place black beans in a large bowl and coarsely mash with a potato masher. Add grated beetroot, mushroom, onion, ginger, garlic, tamari, oil, cumin and chilli; mix well.

3 Process oats and sunflower seeds until they resemble coarse meal. Add to black bean mixture with ground linseeds; mix well.

4 Shape mixture into four patties; place on an oven tray lined with baking paper.

5 Bake patties for 25 minutes, turning halfway through cooking time, or until crisp and brown.

6 Meanwhile, use a julienne peeler, spiraliser or julienne attachment on a mandoline or V-slicer to cut carrot and beetroot into long, thin matchsticks.

7 To make the vegan chilli mayo, combine mayonnaise and sauce in a small bowl; season.

8 Place bun bases on plates and spread with chilli mayo. Spread bun tops with avocado. Top bun bases with salad leaves, patties, carrot, beetroot, cabbage and bun tops. Secure with skewers, if you like.

NUTRITIONAL COUNT PER SERVING protein (22.1g); carbohydrate (60.4g); total fat (42.6g); fibre (19.1g)

LORNA'S TIP Some canned black beans contain added salt, sugar, acetic acid and firming agents, so avoid these. Instead, look for a brand that contains just black beans and water.

CHICKEN SKEWERS
with Kimchi Slaw

PREP + COOK TIME 35 MINUTES SERVES 4

1 tablespoon tamari

1 tablespoon pure maple syrup

1 tablespoon water

600g (1¼lb) organic chicken thigh
fillets, cut into 2.5cm (1in) pieces

2 tablespoons cold-pressed
extra-virgin olive oil

¾ cup (75g) kimchi, shredded finely

2 cups (160g) finely shredded
red cabbage

2 cups (160g) shredded wombok
(chinese cabbage)

⅓ cup (45g) roasted unsalted
peanuts, chopped

1 tablespoon sesame seeds, toasted

mint leaves, to serve

MISO HUMMUS

400g (12½oz) can chickpeas,
drained, rinsed

¼ cup (70g) tahini

2 tablespoons white (shiro)
miso paste

1 clove garlic, crushed

2 tablespoons lemon juice

2 tablespoons cold-pressed
extra-virgin olive oil

1 To make miso hummus, process all ingredients until smooth. Season with pepper.

2 Combine tamari, maple syrup and the water in a medium bowl. Add chicken and mix well to coat in marinade.

3 Thread chicken onto 12 skewers (see Lorna's Tip). Brush the chicken with 1 tablespoon of the oil.

4 Cook skewers on a heated grill plate (or grill or barbecue) over medium-high heat for 2 minutes on each side or until just cooked through. Transfer to a plate; cover to keep warm. Stand for 5 minutes.

5 Meanwhile, combine kimchi, cabbage, wombok and remaining oil in a large bowl.

6 Sprinkle skewers with peanuts and sesame seeds. Serve with miso hummus and kimchi slaw, sprinkled with mint leaves.

NUTRITIONAL COUNT PER SERVING protein (43.7g); carbohydrate (21.4g); total fat (47.1g); fibre (9.8g)

LORNA'S TIP Oil metal skewers before using, or soak bamboo skewers in water for 30 minutes before using to prevent them burning during cooking.

SALMON WITH RED RICE, CABBAGE

& Turmeric Dressing

PREP + COOK TIME 45 MINUTES SERVES 4

½ cup (100g) red rice, rinsed,
drained

1 litre (4 cups) water

2 cups (160g) finely shredded
red or green cabbage

1 tablespoon apple cider vinegar

1 teaspoon pure maple syrup

¼ teaspoon sea salt flakes

½ cup (100g) basmati rice,
rinsed, drained

1½ tablespoons cold-pressed
extra-virgin olive oil

1 bunch asparagus (170g), trimmed,
sliced thinly

4 x 160g (5oz) salmon fillets, skin on,
pin-boned (see Lorna's Tip)

1 tablespoon ground sumac

1 tablespoon sesame seeds

TURMERIC DRESSING

⅓ cup (80ml) hulled tahini

⅓ cup (80ml) warm water

¼ cup (60ml) lemon juice

2 teaspoons pure maple syrup

½ teaspoon ground turmeric

1 Place red rice and the water in a medium
saucepan; bring to boil over high heat. Reduce
heat to low; cook, covered, for 25 minutes.

2 Meanwhile, place cabbage in a bowl with vinegar,
maple syup and salt; toss to combine.

3 To make turmeric dressing, whisk all ingredients
together in a small bowl.

4 Add basmati rice to red rice; cook, covered,
for 10 minutes or until rice is tender. Drain.

5 Heat 1 tablespoon of the oil in a heavy-based
frying pan over medium-high heat. Cook asparagus,
stirring, for 1 minute or until just tender. Transfer
to a plate.

6 Rub salmon with remaining oil and half each
of the sumac and sesame seeds; season. Add salmon
to same pan; cook, skin-side down, pressing firmly,
for 2 minutes. Turn and cook for a further 2 minutes
or until salmon is cooked to your liking.

7 Divide rice mixture, cabbage, asparagus and
salmon among plates or bowls. Drizzle with turmeric
dressing; sprinkle with remaining sumac and seeds.

NUTRITIONAL COUNT PER SERVING protein (54.9g);
carbohydrate (31.4g); total fat (41.8g); fibre (6g)

LORNA'S TIP You can ask the fishmonger to pin-bone
the salmon for you.

MAKE & STASH Turmeric dressing can be made up to
3 days ahead; store in a sealed glass jar in the fridge.

SPICED LAMB WITH

Mint Yoghurt & Quinoa

PREP + COOK TIME 45 MINUTES SERVES 4

200g (6½oz) jap pumpkin, peeled,
  cut into 3cm (1¼in) pieces
1 medium red capsicum (bell pepper)
  (200g), chopped coarsely
¼ cup (60ml) cold-pressed
  extra-virgin olive oil
1 teaspoon cumin seeds
½ cup (40g) flaked almonds
1 cup (200g) white quinoa
2 cups (500ml) water
2 cloves garlic, peeled
2 tablespoons cumin seeds, extra
1 tablespoon coriander seeds
1 bunch coriander (cilantro) (70g)
600g (1¼lb) lamb backstraps
½ cup mint leaves

MINT YOGHURT

½ cup (140g) Greek-style yoghurt
2 tablespoons finely chopped mint leaves
¼ cup (60ml) lime or lemon juice
1 small clove garlic, crushed

1 Preheat oven to 220°C/425°F. Line an
oven tray with baking paper.

2 Place pumpkin and capsicum in a single
layer on lined tray; drizzle with 1 tablespoon
of the oil and sprinkle with cumin seeds.
Season with salt and pepper. Roast for
30 minutes or until golden and tender.

3 Spread almonds on an oven tray and roast
for 3 minutes or until golden.

4 Meanwhile, rinse quinoa under cold water;
drain. Place in a medium saucepan with the
water; bring to boil. Reduce heat; simmer,
covered, for 15 minutes or until water is
absorbed and quinoa is tender.

5 Crush garlic with a pinch of salt in a
mortar and pestle. Add extra cumin and
coriander seeds; crush into a coarse paste.
Transfer to a medium bowl.

6 Pick coriander leaves from stems; reserve.
Clean coriander roots. Finely crush roots
and stems in a mortar and pestle. Add
2 tablespoons of the crushed coriander
to the spice paste along with 1 cup of the
reserved coriander leaves, chopped finely.
Stir in remaining oil; season well with salt
and freshly ground black pepper. Add lamb;
toss to evenly coat.

7 Cook lamb on a lightly oiled grill plate
(or grill or barbecue) on medium-high heat
for 4 minutes each side or until cooked to
your liking. Transfer lamb to a plate; cover
and stand for 5 minutes, then slice thickly.

8 To make mint yoghurt, combine all
ingredients in a bowl.

9 Divide quinoa among plates; top with
vegetables, lamb, almonds, ¼ cup of the
reserved coriander leaves and the mint.
Serve with mint yoghurt.

NUTRITIONAL COUNT PER SERVING
protein (43.3g); carbohydrate (44.8g);
total fat (31.3g); fibre (7.3g)

SOCCA PIZZA WITH ZUCCHINI, Tomato & Goat's Cheese

PREP + COOK TIME 45 MINUTES (+ STANDING) MAKES 4

2 cups (300g) chickpea flour (besan)
  (see Lorna's Tips)
1 teaspoon garlic powder
2⅓ cups (580ml) water
¼ cup (60ml) cold-pressed
  extra-virgin olive oil
3 heirloom tomatoes (420g)
  (see Lorna's Tips)
1 small clove garlic, crushed
2 tablespoons shredded basil leaves
2 medium zucchini (240g),
  sliced thinly
200g (6½oz) goat's cheese
2 cups (35g) baby rocket (arugula)
2 tablespoons finely grated
  parmesan
2 teaspoons cold-pressed
  extra-virgin olive oil, extra

1 Combine chickpea flour and garlic powder
in a large jug; season. Whisk in the water and oil;
stand for 30 minutes.

2 Meanwhile, preheat oven to 240°C/475°F.
Line two large oven trays with baking paper.

3 Blend or process 1 chopped tomato with garlic
until smooth. Stir in basil; season.

4 Heat a greased 27cm (10¾in) wide, 20cm (8in)
(base measurement), frying pan over medium heat.
Add ¼ of the chickpea mixture to the pan. Cook for
5 minutes or until cooked through and base is golden
and crisp. Slide base out of pan onto tray, browned-
side down. Repeat to make four bases in total. Two
bases should fit on one large tray.

5 Spread bases with tomato mixture. Slice remaining
tomatoes. Top bases with zucchini, sliced tomato and
crumbled goat's cheese.

6 Bake pizzas for 12 minutes or until golden and
crisp. Top with rocket and parmesan; drizzle with
extra oil. Serve sprinkled with extra basil leaves,
if you like.

NUTRITIONAL COUNT PER PIZZA protein (29.2g);
carbohydrate (40.7g); total fat (32.8g); fibre (10.4g)

LORNA'S TIPS Chickpea flour is available from some
supermarkets and health food stores. You can use
ripe truss tomatoes in place of heirloom, if you like.
This recipe can be made, to the end of step 4, several
hours ahead. Keep bases in an airtight container and
the tomato mixture in the fridge.

CHICKEN WITH *Watermelon Salad*

PREP + COOK TIME 35 MINUTES SERVES 4

¼ cup (60ml) white vinegar

½ cup (125ml) cold-pressed
extra-virgin olive oil

1 clove garlic, crushed

1 tablespoon grated ginger

½ cup basil leaves, shredded finely

4 x 250g (8oz) skinless organic
chicken breast fillets

600g (1¼lb) watermelon,
peeled, chopped

4 baby cucumbers (qukes) (120g),
sliced (see Lorna's Tip)

½ small red onion (50g), sliced thinly

⅓ cup (55g) dry-roasted almonds,
chopped

½ cup mint sprigs

1 Preheat oven to 200°C/400°F.

2 Process vinegar, oil, garlic, ginger and basil in
a small food processor until smooth. Season to taste.
Reserve half the basil mixture.

3 Place chicken in a shallow non-reactive dish.
Pour over the remaining basil mixture; turn to coat.

4 Heat an ovenproof frying pan or flameproof
baking dish over medium-high heat. Cook chicken
for 5 minutes or until golden. Turn chicken; season.
Transfer pan to oven. Roast chicken for 12 minutes
or until just cooked through. Transfer to a plate;
cover loosely. Rest chicken for 5 minutes.

5 Meanwhile, combine watermelon, cucumber,
onion, almonds and mint in a bowl. Drizzle chicken
with reserved basil mixture; serve with salad.

NUTRITIONAL COUNT PER SERVING protein (59.4g);
carbohydrate (9.6g); total fat (40.6g); fibre (2.9g)

LORNA'S TIP For shape and texture, I slice the
cucumbers into ribbons, rounds and matchsticks.

POACHED CHICKEN WITH
Avocado & Quinoa Salad

PREP + COOK TIME 30 MINUTES (+ COOLING) SERVES 4

500g (1lb) organic chicken breast
  fillets, trimmed
2 cups (500ml) chicken stock
1 cup (200g) tri-coloured quinoa
2 cups (500ml) water
1 tablespoon linseeds (flaxseeds)
1 tablespoon sesame seeds, toasted
2 cups (60g) watercress sprigs
6 trimmed radishes (90g),
  sliced thinly
1 small avocado (200g),
  cut into wedges
¼ cup (50g) pepitas
  (pumpkin seed kernels)
MAPLE DIJON DRESSING
¼ cup (60ml) cold-pressed
  extra-virgin olive oil
2 tablespoons red wine vinegar
1 teaspoon pure maple syrup
2 teaspoons dijon mustard

1 Place chicken in a medium saucepan with chicken stock; bring just to boil. Reduce heat to low; simmer, uncovered, for 10 minutes or until cooked through. Cool chicken in poaching liquid for 10 minutes; drain. Slice chicken.

2 Meanwhile, rinse quinoa well; drain. Place quinoa and the water in a medium saucepan; bring to boil. Reduce heat to low; simmer, covered, for 10 minutes or until quinoa is tender. Rinse quinoa in a sieve under cold running water. Drain, pressing quinoa with the back of a spoon to remove as much water as possible. Transfer to a medium bowl; stir in seeds. Season to taste.

3 To make maple dijon dressing, stir ingredients in a small jug; season to taste.

4 Place quinoa and chicken in a large bowl with remaining ingredients; drizzle with dressing.

NUTRITIONAL COUNT PER SERVING protein (40.7g); carbohydrate (36.9g); total fat (34.7g); fibre (6.5g)

Our health is our wealth — and we should all be eating good food, exercising regularly and living positive and uplifting lives.

TOM YUM PRAWN
Broccoli 'Fried Rice'

PREP + COOK TIME 30 MINUTES SERVES 4

2 tablespoons tom yum paste

2 tablespoons lime juice

1 tablespoon finely grated ginger

1 long red chilli, sliced thinly

1 clove garlic, crushed

500g (1lb) large uncooked prawns

1 tablespoon cold-pressed
extra-virgin coconut oil

2 free-range eggs, beaten lightly

500g (1lb) broccoli, cut into florets,
stems chopped

4 green onions (scallions),
sliced thinly

1 medium carrot (120g), cut into
thin matchsticks

½ cup (75g) roasted cashews,
chopped

⅓ cup coriander (cilantro) leaves

1 lime, cut into wedges

1 Whisk paste, juice, ginger, chilli and garlic in a medium bowl. Peel and devein prawns, leaving tails intact. Add prawns to bowl; toss to combine in paste mixture.

2 Heat 1 teaspoon of the coconut oil in a wok over high heat. Pour egg into wok; cook, tilting wok to spread egg, until almost set. Remove omelette from wok; roll tightly into a cigar shape and slice thinly.

3 Place broccoli in a food processor; pulse until finely chopped and resembling rice.

4 Heat remaining coconut oil in wok over high heat. Add green onion and carrot; stir-fry for 5 minutes or until tender. Add prawn mixture; stir-fry for 5 minutes or until just cooked. Add broccoli and stir-fry for a further 2 minutes.

5 Top 'fried rice' with cashews and coriander. Serve with sliced omelette and lime wedges.

NUTRITIONAL COUNT PER SERVING protein (26.3g); carbohydrate (10.9g); total fat (20.1g); fibre (7.7g)

POLENTA-CRUSTED FISH WITH
Parsnip Mash & Salsa

PREP + COOK TIME 30 MINUTES SERVES 4

1kg (2lb) parsnips, peeled,
  chopped coarsely
1 cup (170g) polenta
1 teaspoon ground cumin
4 x 200g (6½oz) skinless boneless
  blue-eye trevalla fillets
  (see Lorna's Tip)
¼ cup (60ml) cold-pressed
  extra-virgin olive oil
200g (6½oz) green beans, trimmed
1 lime

TOMATO LIME SALSA
1 large tomato (220g),
  chopped coarsely
¼ medium red onion (40g),
  chopped finely
1 tablespoon coarsely chopped
  coriander (cilantro)
2 teaspoons lime juice
1 tablespoon cold-pressed
  extra-virgin olive oil

1 Bring a large saucepan of water to boil. Add parsnip; boil for 15 minutes or until tender. Drain.

2 Meanwhile, to make tomato lime salsa, combine all ingredients in a small bowl. Season to taste with salt and pepper.

3 Combine polenta and cumin in a wide bowl. Toss fish in the polenta mixture; transfer to a plate. Season with salt and pepper.

4 Using a potato masher, mash parsnip with 2 tablespoons of the oil. Season to taste. Keep warm.

5 Heat a large non-stick frying pan over medium heat. Add remaining oil; cook fish for 2 minutes each side or until golden and just cooked through. (Cooking time will vary depending on the thickness of the fish.)

6 Cook beans in a saucepan of boiling water for 3 minutes or until just tender. Drain. Finely grate a little lime rind over beans, if you like. Cut lime into wedges.

7 Divide mash among plates; top with fish and salsa. Serve with lime wedges and beans.

NUTRITIONAL COUNT PER SERVING protein (46.1g); carbohydrate (57.4g); total fat (21.4g); fibre (12.3g)

LORNA'S TIP You can use your favourite white fish, such as snapper, perch, barramundi, cod or ling.

PULLED FISH & SLAW *Tortillas*

PREP + COOK TIME 30 MINUTES SERVES 4

3 teaspoons Tabasco chipotle sauce

2 tablespoons red wine vinegar

2 teaspoons pure maple syrup

¼ small red cabbage (200g), shredded finely

1 bunch coriander (cilantro) (70g)

600g (1¼lb) skinless, boneless white fish fillets (see Lorna's Tips)

2 tablespoons cold-pressed extra-virgin olive oil

8 small stone-ground blue corn tortillas (200g) (see Lorna's Tips)

1 lime, halved

1 Preheat oven to 200°C/400°F. Line an oven tray with baking paper.

2 Whisk ½ teaspoon Tabasco, the vinegar and maple syrup in a large bowl. Add cabbage; toss gently to combine. Season well.

3 Pick coriander sprigs from stems; reserve. Clean coriander roots; process roots and stems in a small food processor until chopped finely. Place fish on lined tray; spread coriander mixture on both sides and drizzle with olive oil. Season.

4 Bake fish for 10 minutes or until just cooked through. Wrap tortillas in foil; heat in the oven on a separate shelf for 10 minutes.

5 Using two forks, pull fish apart, flaking it into large pieces.

6 Serve warm tortillas topped with red slaw, pulled fish and reserved coriander sprigs; drizzle with remaining Tabasco. Serve with lime.

NUTRITIONAL COUNT PER SERVING protein (35.2g); carbohydrate (23.3g); total fat (13.3g); fibre (5.5g)

LORNA'S TIPS You can use white fish such as whiting, snapper, bream, perch, barramundi, cod or ling. Stone-ground blue corn tortillas are available from specialty food stores or online.

SWEET POTATO *Frittata*

PREP + COOK TIME 45 MINUTES SERVES 6

2 tablespoons cold-pressed
extra-virgin olive oil

1 medium brown onion (150g),
sliced thinly

300g (9½oz) orange sweet potato,
peeled, sliced very thinly

12 free-range eggs, beaten lightly

250g (8oz) fresh ricotta

1 tablespoon harissa paste

1 tablespoon sunflower seed kernels

2 tablespoons coarsely chopped
natural almonds

¼ cup coriander (cilantro) leaves

1 Heat half the oil in a 24cm (9½in)
(top measurement) ovenproof frying pan over
medium heat. Add onion and sweet potato;
carefully stir to coat in oil. Season. Reduce heat
to low. Cover; cook for 20 minutes or until tender.

2 Preheat a grill (broiler) to high.

3 Transfer sweet potato mixture to a large bowl.
Add egg; stir well to coat. Heat remaining oil
in same pan over medium heat. Add egg mixture.
Reduce heat to very low; cook for 10 minutes or until
partially set. Place under grill; cook for 5 minutes or
until golden and cooked through. Stand for 5 minutes.

4 Serve frittata topped with ricotta, harissa,
sunflower seeds, almonds and coriander.

NUTRITIONAL COUNT PER SERVING protein (21.3g);
carbohydrate (12.7g); total fat (22.4g); fibre (2.2g)

PICK-YOUR-PROTEIN Curry

PREP + COOK TIME 30 MINUTES SERVES 4

2 tablespoons cold-pressed
    extra-virgin coconut oil
2 cloves garlic, chopped
1 tablespoon grated ginger
¼ cup (75g) thai red curry paste
1 medium orange sweet potato
    (400g), peeled, grated coarsely
1 cup (250ml) canned coconut milk
2 cups (500ml) stock of choice
    (see Lorna's Tip)
600g (1¼lb) protein of choice, cut
    into pieces (see Pick Your Protein)
100g (3oz) broccolini, cut into florets
1 medium red capsicum (bell pepper)
    (200g), sliced
120g (4oz) green beans, halved
½ cup coriander (cilantro) leaves
1 lime, cut into wedges

1 Heat oil in a large saucepan over low heat.
Cook garlic, ginger, curry paste and sweet potato,
stirring, for 5 minutes or until sweet potato is tender.
Stir in coconut milk and stock. Blend or process,
in batches, until smooth.

2 Return curry to pan; bring to a simmer.
Add protein and vegetables; simmer for 5 minutes
or until protein is cooked through and vegetables
are just tender. Season to taste.

3 Sprinkle curry with coriander leaves; serve with
lime wedges and steamed rice or cauliflower rice
(see page 187), if you like.

PICK YOUR PROTEIN In this recipe I used 300g (9½oz)
skinless firm white fish fillets and 300g (9½oz) peeled
uncooked prawns, deveined and with tails intact.
If you peel the prawns yourself, you will need to buy
about 600g (1¼lb) king prawns in the shell to yield
300g (9½oz). You could use 600g (1¼lb) of sliced
chicken breast fillets, sliced lamb backstrap (eye of
loin), sliced pork scotch fillet, sliced rump steak or
chopped tofu.

NUTRITIONAL COUNT PER SERVING protein (38.5g);
carbohydrate (25.1g); total fat (24.7g); fibre (5.8g)

LORNA'S TIP Use good-quality homemade or
purchased liquid stock to match the protein.

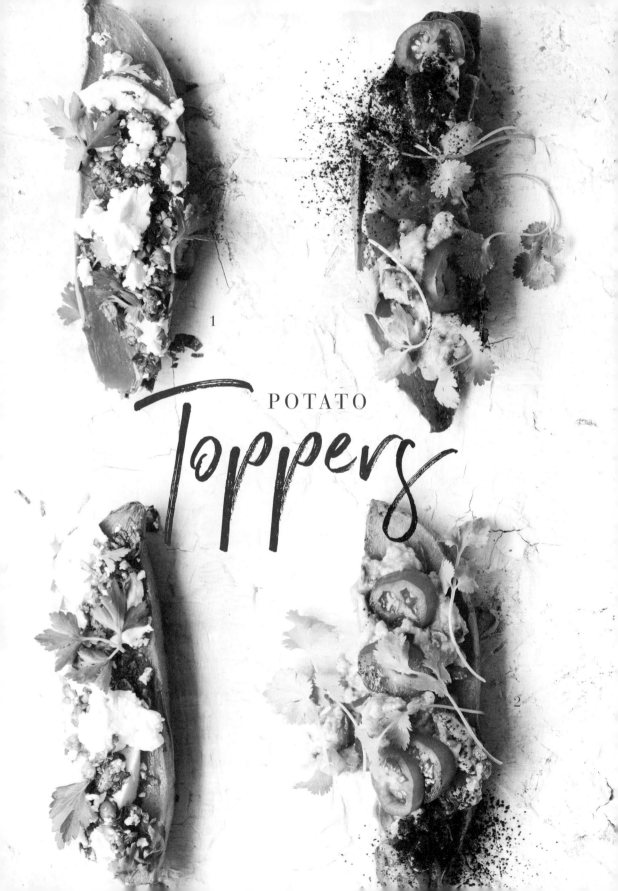

POTATO

Toppers

1

2

3

ROAST SWEET POTATOES

PREP + COOK TIME 50 MINUTES SERVES 4

Preheat oven to 180°C/350°F. Wash 4 small
sweet potatoes (1kg); pat dry. Prick the skin in
several places with a skewer. Place on an oven
tray. Bake for 45 minutes or until tender.
Cut potatoes in half lengthways.

Topping variations

SALSA VERDE

Chop 1 cup each lightly packed basil and flat-leaf
parsley; transfer to a bowl. Chop 1 clove garlic,
2 anchovy fillets and 2 teaspoons capers. Add to
bowl with 2 tablespoons extra-virgin olive oil and
1 teaspoon lemon juice. Season. Crumble 150g
(4½oz) goat's cheese; spread half over roast sweet
potato halves; top with salsa verde and remaining
cheese. Scatter with extra flat-leaf parsely.

SUPERFOOD GUACAMOLE

Mash 2 medium avocados (500g) in a medium
bowl with 1 small finely chopped red chilli,
1 clove crushed garlic and 1 tablespoon lime
juice; season. Spoon onto roast sweet potato
halves; top with 8 sliced grape tomatoes and
sprinkle with ¼ teaspoon spirulina. Scatter with
½ cup fresh coriander (cilantro) leaves.

CHILLI BLACK BEANS

Drain and rinse a 400g (12½oz) can black beans.
Heat 2 tablespoons extra-virgin olive oil in a
frying pan over medium heat; cook 2 crushed
cloves garlic and beans, crushing the beans, for
2 minutes; season to taste. Char-grill 1 corn cob
(250g), turning, for 8 minutes; cut corn from cob.
Spoon bean mixture and corn onto roast sweet
potato halves; sprinkle with 2 sliced green onions
(scallions) and drizzle with a little chilli sauce.

PARSNIP NOODLES WITH *Meatballs*

PREP + COOK TIME 40 MINUTES SERVES 4

500g (1lb) lean minced (ground)
   grass-fed beef

2 cloves garlic, crushed

1 medium carrot (120g), grated finely

1 free-range egg, beaten lightly

2 tablespoons rolled oats

¼ cup (60ml) cold-pressed
   extra-virgin olive oil

1 medium brown onion (150g),
   chopped finely

2 cloves garlic, extra, chopped finely

2 tablespoons no-added-sugar
   tomato paste

2 cups (500ml) chicken or beef stock

400g (12½oz) can diced tomatoes

6 large parsnips (2kg), trimmed

¼ cup (20g) finely grated pecorino
   or parmesan

¼ cup basil leaves

1 Combine beef, garlic, carrot and egg in a bowl; season. Process oats until chopped finely. Add to bowl; mix well. Roll tablespoonfuls of mixture into balls.

2 Heat 1 tablespoon of the oil in a large deep frying pan over medium-high heat. Cook meatballs, shaking pan occasionally, for 4 minutes or until browned all over. Remove from pan.

3 Heat another 1 tablespoon of the oil in same pan over medium heat. Cook onion and extra garlic, stirring occasionally, for 5 minutes or until softened. Stir in paste; cook, stirring, for 1 minute. Add stock and tomatoes; bring to boil. Return meatballs to pan; reduce heat to low. Simmer for 10 minutes or until sauce thickens. Season.

4 Using a spiraliser (see Lorna's Tips), cut parsnips into thick noodles. Heat remaining oil in a separate large deep frying pan with a lid over medium heat. Add parsnip; cook, covered, for 5 minutes or until just tender. Season to taste.

5 Serve parsnip noodles with meatballs and sauce, topped with pecorino and basil.

NUTRITIONAL COUNT PER SERVING protein (47.3g); carbohydrate (56.9g); total fat (29g); fibre (20.9g

LORNA'S TIPS A spiraliser is a kitchen gadget that cuts vegetables to resemble noodles. You can use a julienne peeler or a julienne attachment on a mandoline or V-slicer. Parsnip noodles are best made just before serving. The sauce can be made a day ahead; store in an airtight container in the fridge.

MAKE & STASH Sauce can be frozen for up to 2 months.

AYURVEDIC BEEF CURRY WITH
Cauliflower Rice & Raita

PREP + COOK TIME 2 HOURS 30 MINUTES SERVES 6

2½ teaspoons ground turmeric

2 teaspoons ground cumin

1½ teaspoons ground coriander

½ teaspoon ground cardamom

¼ teaspoon ground chilli

1 teaspoon ground black pepper

1 teaspoon fennel seeds

1 teaspoon fenugreek seeds

2 tablespoons ghee or cold-pressed
extra-virgin coconut oil

2 large brown onions (400g),
chopped coarsely

2 large cloves garlic, crushed

1 tablespoon grated ginger

3 sprigs fresh curry leaves

1½ tablespoons apple cider vinegar

2 teaspoons fine sea salt

1.5kg (3lb) lean grass-fed
beef chuck steak, trimmed,
cut into 5cm (2in) cubes

4 medium tomatoes (600g),
chopped coarsely

2 tablespoons finely chopped
mint leaves

1 teaspoon garam masala

⅓ cup coriander or mint leaves

1 lemon, cut into wedges

CAULIFLOWER RICE

1 medium cauliflower (1.5kg),
cut into florets

1½ tablespoons cold-pressed
extra-virgin olive oil

½ teaspoon ground cinnamon

MINT RAITA

1 lebanese cucumber (130g), grated

1 cup (280g) Greek-style yoghurt

2 tablespoons finely chopped mint leaves

2 tablespoons lemon juice

1 small clove garlic, crushed

1 Combine dry spices and seeds in a small bowl.

2 Heat ghee in a large heavy-based saucepan over low-medium heat; cook onion, stirring, for 8 minutes or until translucent. Add garlic, ginger and curry leaves; cook, stirring, for 1 minute or until onion is soft.

3 Add spice mix; cook, stirring, for 1 minute or until fragrant. Stir in vinegar and salt. Add beef; cook, stirring, for 2 minutes or until coated in the spices. Stir in tomato and mint; bring to boil.

4 Reduce heat to low; simmer, covered, stirring occasionally, for 2 hours or until beef is fork-tender. Stir in garam masala; simmer, uncovered, for a further 10 minutes or until sauce thickens.

5 Meanwhile, to make the cauliflower rice, preheat oven to 200°C/400°F. Line an oven tray with baking paper. Process cauliflower until finely chopped and resembling rice; transfer to a bowl and toss with oil and cinnamon. Spread cauliflower over tray. Roast for 20 minutes, stirring halfway, or until golden and soft.

6 To make the raita, squeeze excess liquid from cucumber. Combine cucumber with remaining ingredients in a small bowl; season to taste.

7 Sprinkle curry with coriander leaves; serve with cauliflower rice, mint raita and lemon wedges.

NUTRITIONAL COUNT PER SERVING protein (56.4g); carbohydrate (10.6g); total fat (23.9g); fibre (7.9g)

SALMON WITH ROASTED
Sprouts & Crisp Capers

PREP + COOK TIME 30 MINUTES SERVES 4

¼ cup (35g) slivered almonds

2 tablespoons cold-pressed
   extra-virgin olive oil

700g (1½lb) brussels sprouts,
   trimmed, halved (or quartered
   if large)

2 tablespoons baby capers

4 x 150g (4½oz) salmon fillets,
   pin-boned, skin on

1 lemon, cut into wedges

YOGHURT HERB SAUCE

⅔ cup (190g) Greek-style yoghurt

2 tablespoons chopped dill

2 tablespoons chopped chives

1 clove garlic, crushed

1 Preheat oven to 180°C/350°F. Line an oven tray with baking paper.

2 Place almonds on lined tray; roast for 6 minutes or until golden. Transfer to a small bowl. Put oven tray aside for roasting sprouts.

3 Heat half the oil in a large non-stick frying pan over medium heat; cook sprouts for 3 minutes or until lightly golden. Season. Transfer to tray; roast for 10 minutes or until tender. Put pan aside for frying capers and salmon.

4 Meanwhile, to make yoghurt herb sauce, combine all ingredients in a small bowl. Season to taste.

5 Pat capers dry with paper towel. Heat remaining oil in frying pan over medium-high heat; cook capers, stirring frequently, for 2 minutes or until crisp (take care as the oil will splatter while cooking). Remove with a slotted spoon; drain on paper towel.

6 Pat salmon dry with paper towel. Using a sharp knife, make three 6cm (2½in) cuts in the thickest part of each fillet; season with salt. Cook fillets, skin-side down, in same frying pan over medium heat for 5 minutes or until golden and crisp. Turn; cook for a further 2 minutes or until done as desired.

7 Serve salmon with brussels sprouts, almonds, capers, yoghurt herb sauce and lemon wedges; sprinkle with extra chopped dill, if you like.

NUTRITIONAL COUNT PER SERVING protein (53.4g); carbohydrate (11.8g); total fat (36.3g); fibre (8.9g)

GREEN MASALA CHICKEN *Curry*

PREP + COOK TIME 50 MINUTES SERVES 6

2 bunches coriander (cilantro)
  (140g), roots, stems and
  leaves chopped coarsely
  (see Lorna's Tips)
1 cup mint leaves
120g (4oz) baby spinach leaves
1 long green chilli, seeded, chopped
4 cloves garlic, chopped
¼ cup (60ml) lemon juice
¼ cup (60ml) water
2 tablespoons cold-pressed
  extra-virgin coconut oil
1 medium brown onion (150g),
  sliced
1kg (2lb) skinless organic chicken
  breast fillets, sliced or chopped
1½ teaspoons ground turmeric
½ teaspoon ground cinnamon
½ teaspoon ground cardamom
¼ teaspoon ground cloves
1 cup (250ml) canned coconut cream
40g (1½oz) baby spinach leaves
⅓ cup (25g) flaked almonds, roasted
1 lime, cut into wedges

1 Reserve a handful of coriander leaves and mint leaves for serving. Blend or process remaining coriander and mint with spinach, chilli, garlic, juice and the water until smooth.

2 Heat oil in a large deep frying pan over medium-high heat; cook onion, stirring, for 5 minutes or until starting to brown. Add chicken in batches; cook for 5 minutes or until chicken is browned lightly. Add spices; cook, stirring, for 1 minute or until fragrant.

3 Stir in coriander puree and coconut cream; bring to boil. Reduce heat to low; simmer for 5 minutes. Return chicken to pan; simmer for another 5 minutes or until sauce thickens slightly and chicken is cooked through. Season to taste.

4 Top curry with extra spinach, almonds, and reserved coriander and mint; serve with lime wedges.

NUTRITIONAL COUNT PER SERVING protein (41g); carbohydrate (5.1g); total fat (19.7g); fibre (3.4g)

LORNA'S TIPS Wash coriander thoroughly before chopping. For a great vegie curry, swap the chicken for chopped vegetables such as sweet potato or cauliflower, and drained and rinsed chickpeas (garbanzo beans) or lentils. Simmer until tender. For the Eating Plan to Cleanse on pages 16–17, swap the chicken for vegetables.

SERVING SUGGESTIONS Serve with steamed rice or the cauliflower rice from page 187.

Dressings

1

3

MAPLE & DIJON DRESSING

Whisk ¼ cup macadamia or extra-virgin olive oil,
¼ cup apple cider vinegar, 2 tablespoons pure
maple syrup and 1 tablespoon dijon mustard
in a small bowl until combined. Season to taste.
Makes ⅔ cup. Keeps refrigerated for 1 month.
Serve with leafy salads.

KIMCHI DRESSING

Blend or process 1 cup yoghurt, 2 tablespoons
extra-virgin olive oil, 2 tablespoons chopped
kimchi, ½ crushed garlic clove, 1 tablespoon
lemon juice and 3 teaspoons white (shiro)
miso paste until smooth. Season. Makes 1⅔ cups.
Keeps refrigerated for 1 week. Serve with leafy
salads, or on steamed potatoes, grilled chicken,
beef or lamb.

BLACKBERRY & WHITE BALSAMIC VINAIGRETTE

Push ½ cup fresh or thawed frozen blackberries
through a fine sieve into a small bowl using
the back of a spoon. Whisk in ¼ cup white
balsamic vinegar, 2 tablespoons macadamia oil
and 1 teaspoon norbu (monk fruit sugar) or stevia
granules. Season to taste. Makes ⅔ cup. Keeps
refrigerated for 1 week. Serve with leafy salads
or grilled pork.

LEMONY AVOCADO & DILL DRESSING

Blend or process 1 medium (250g) avocado,
¼ cup Greek-style yoghurt, 2 tablespoons avocado
oil, ⅓ cup water, ⅓ cup dill sprigs and ¼ cup
lemon juice until smooth. Season to taste.
Makes 1½ cups. Keeps refrigerated for 1 week.
Serve with salads, roast chicken or cold prawns.

EGGPLANT & ZUCCHINI *Lasagne*

PREP + COOK TIME 1 HOUR 30 MINUTES (+ COOLING) SERVES 6

⅓ cup (80ml) cold-pressed
   extra-virgin olive oil
2 medium eggplants (600g)
3 large zucchini (450g)
200g (7oz) fresh shiitake mushrooms,
   stems discarded, chopped finely
2 tablespoons finely chopped sage
1 teaspoon smoked paprika
400g (12½oz) can chopped tomatoes
125g (4oz) sun-dried tomatoes,
   chopped finely (see Lorna's Tips)
¾ cup (90g) walnuts, chopped finely
1 cup (250ml) tomato passata
1 cup (250ml) vegetable stock
¼ cup (20g) finely grated parmesan

CAULIFLOWER BÉCHAMEL
¾ head cauliflower (750g), cut into florets
3 cloves garlic, bruised
1½ cups (375ml) vegetable stock
375g (12oz) fresh ricotta
¾ cup (60g) finely grated parmesan
¼ teaspoon ground nutmeg

1 Preheat oven grill to high. Line a large oven tray with foil; brush with a little oil.

2 Cut eggplants and zucchini lengthways into 4mm (⅛in) thick slices.

3 Cooking in batches, place eggplant in a single layer on oiled tray; brush with 1 tablespoon of the oil. Season. Grill for 5 minutes each side or until golden. Repeat with zucchini slices and another 1 tablespoon of oil; grill for 3 minutes each side until golden.

4 Preheat oven to 200°C/400°F.

5 To make cauliflower béchamel, place cauliflower, garlic and stock in a medium saucepan over medium heat; bring to a simmer. Reduce heat to low; cook, covered, for 12 minutes or until cauliflower is tender. Cool for 10 minutes. Blend or process with cheeses and nutmeg until smooth; season.

6 Meanwhile, heat 1 tablespoon of the oil in a frying pan over medium-high heat. Cook mushroom for 2 minutes. Add sage and paprika; cook for a further 3 minutes or until golden. Stir in canned and sun-dried tomatoes, walnuts, passata and stock. Bring to a simmer; simmer for 12 minutes or until thickened slightly. Season to taste.

7 Spread a quarter of the cauliflower béchamel in a 2.5-litre (10-cup) rectangular baking dish. Arrange a layer of vegetables on top. Top with another quarter of the béchamel. Spoon over half the sun-dried tomato mixture. Repeat layering with vegetables, béchamel and tomato mixture, finishing with a béchamel layer. Top with parmesan. Drizzle with remaining oil; season with salt and pepper.

8 Bake for 20 minutes or until top is golden and filling heated through.

NUTRITIONAL COUNT PER SERVING protein (21.7g); carbohydrate (21.9); total fat (33.2); fibre (13.1)

LORNA'S TIPS Make sure you purchase sun-dried tomatoes without brine, oil or any other liquid, as you need the dried version for this recipe to soak up some of the vegetable juices released during cooking. You can fry any leftover sage leaves in a little oil until crisp, then use to garnish the lasagne, if you like.

SMOKY BEAN & BEEF BALLS
in Lettuce Wraps

PREP + COOK TIME 40 MINUTES (+ REFRIGERATION) SERVES 6

300g (9½oz) lean minced (ground)
  grass-fed beef
400g (12½oz) can red kidney beans,
  drained, rinsed, mashed coarsely
1 teaspoon smoked paprika
1 teaspoon ground cumin
¼ cup (30g) coarsely grated cheddar
1 medium red onion (170g),
  grated coarsely
1 clove garlic, crushed
1 free-range egg
1 cup (70g) crushed gluten-free
  plain rice crackers
1 tablespoon cold-pressed
  extra-virgin olive oil
4 small ripe tomatoes (360g),
  chopped
2 tablespoons coriander
  (cilantro) leaves
2 small avocados (400g)
1 tablespoon lime juice
6 baby cos (romaine) lettuce leaves

1 Combine beef, beans, paprika, cumin, cheddar, onion, garlic, egg and crackers in a large bowl; season. Shape mixture into 12 balls. Refrigerate for 30 minutes or until firm.

2 Heat oil in a large frying pan over medium heat; cook balls for 8 minutes, shaking pan occasionally, until browned and cooked through. Remove from heat; cover to keep warm.

3 Meanwhile, combine tomato and coriander in a small bowl; season to taste.

4 Mash avocado and juice together in a medium bowl until smooth and creamy; season.

5 Serve balls in lettuce leaves with mashed avocado and tomato mixture.

NUTRITIONAL COUNT PER SERVING protein (21.4g); carbohydrate (18.7g); total fat (18.2g); fibre (5.7g)

LORNA'S TIP The balls can be made, to the end of step 1, a day ahead.

MAKE & STASH Beef balls can be frozen for up to 2 months.

LAMB & BUCKWHEAT *Koftas*

PREP + COOK TIME 50 MINUTES (+ REFRIGERATION) SERVES 4

¼ cup (50g) buckwheat

300g (9½oz) lean minced (ground) lamb (see Lorna's Tips)

200g (6½oz) lean minced (ground) grass-fed beef

1 teaspoon ground cinnamon

1 teaspoon ground allspice

1 teaspoon ground black pepper

1 medium brown onion (150g), grated coarsely

2 cloves garlic, crushed

4 free-range eggs

1 medium eggplant (300g), sliced thinly lengthways

¼ cup (60ml) cold-pressed extra-virgin olive oil

100g (3oz) mixed salad leaves

¼ cup flat-leaf parsley leaves

⅓ cup (70g) Greek-style yoghurt

1 tablespoon pomegranate molasses

1 medium pomegranate (320g), seeds removed (see Lorna's Tips)

1 teaspoon ground sumac

1 Cook buckwheat in a small saucepan of boiling water for 15 minutes or until just tender. Drain; rinse under cold water; drain.

2 Combine buckwheat, lamb, beef, spices, onion and garlic in a large bowl; season well. Shape heaped tablespoonfuls of mixture into ovals; place on a tray. Cover; refrigerate for 30 minutes until firm.

3 Meanwhile, place eggs in a small saucepan and cover with cold water; bring to boil. Boil for 4 minutes; drain. Peel shell; cut in half.

4 Toss eggplant in 2 tablespoons of the oil to coat; season. Cook eggplant on a heated grill plate or barbecue over medium-high heat for 5 minutes or until browned on both sides and cooked through. Cover to keep warm.

5 Brush remaining oil over koftas. Cook koftas on a heated grill plate for 8 minutes or until browned all over and cooked through.

6 Serve koftas with salad leaves, parsley, eggplant and egg. Drizzle with yoghurt and pomegranate molasses; sprinkle with pomegranate seeds and sumac. Season to taste.

NUTRITIONAL COUNT PER SERVING protein (42.1g); carbohydrate (24.8g); total fat (35.6g); fibre (9.2g)

LORNA'S TIPS You can ask the butcher to mince some lamb for you that is leaner than regular minced lamb. To remove seeds from pomegranate, cut in half crossways; hold, cut-side down, in the palm of your hand over a bowl, then hit the outside firmly with a wooden spoon. The seeds should fall out easily; discard any white pith that falls out with them. Koftas can be prepared a day ahead; keep covered in the fridge.

MAKE & STASH Koftas can be frozen for up to 3 months.

THE SWEET
STUFF

I LOVE dessert and there's no way in my quest for good health
that I could seriously think about not having a little sweet treat
at the end of my day. I think it's important to eat foods that excite
you, so when it came to deciding on dessert recipes for this book
I wanted to make them super-delicious but still light, bright,
fresh and nutritious enough to incorporate into your healthy
eating plan. The ones that made the cut are, in my opinion,
pretty spectacular – many of them are gluten-free, sugar-free
or dairy-free. Most of them are jam-packed with fresh fruit –
and the passionfruit cheesecake even has a vegetable in it for
good measure! Welcome to my world – where you can have
a little indulgence at the end of your day and know that it's
going to be good for your health as well!

COCONUT, BERRY MERINGUE *Sandwiches*

PREP + COOK TIME 3 HOURS (+ OVERNIGHT REFRIGERATION & COOLING) MAKES 8

400g (12½oz) can coconut cream
1 cup (220g) pure maple sugar
   (see Lorna's Tips)
4 free-range egg whites
2 teaspoons tapioca starch
   (see Lorna's Tips)
1 teaspoon white vinegar
2 teaspoons pure vanilla extract
80g (2½oz) fresh raspberries
80g (2½oz) fresh blackberries

1 Chill coconut cream can overnight in the fridge so that cream separates and sets on top. Keep the can upright.

2 Heat oven to 140°C/275°F. Line two large oven trays with baking paper.

3 Blend maple sugar in a high-powered blender until a fine powder; sift powdered maple sugar into a bowl.

4 Beat egg whites in a small bowl with an electric mixer until soft peaks form. Gradually add sugar, one tablespoon at a time. Once all the sugar has been added, scrape down the sides of bowl with a spatula and keep beating until sugar dissolves and mixture is stiff, thick and glossy. Beat in tapioca starch and vinegar. Spoon ¼ cupfuls of meringue mixture onto trays, about 5cm (2in) apart, to make 16 meringues in total.

5 Bake meringues for 15 minutes. Reduce heat to 120°C/250°F. Bake for 2½ hours or until meringues are crisp, dry to touch and lift easily from the baking paper. Cool in the oven with the door slightly ajar to allow meringues to dry out completely.

6 Without shaking or tipping the can of coconut cream, carefully spoon out the thick cream that has set on top. Beat cream and vanilla in a small bowl with an electric mixer until soft peaks form.

7 Place berries in two separate small bowls and mash with a fork.

8 Spread bases of eight meringues with whipped cream; top with seperate berries (or combine them if you like) and remaining meringues. Serve straight away.

NUTRITIONAL COUNT PER MERINGUE SANDWICH
protein (2.9g); carbohydrate (31.9g); total fat (9.5g); fibre (1.2g)

LORNA'S TIPS Pure maple sugar is available from some health food stores. It is a healthy alternative sweetener made entirely from pure maple syrup. You can use raw caster sugar, if you prefer. Tapioca starch is a healthy substitute for cornflour (cornstarch) when baking. You can swap whipped coconut cream with vanilla coconut yoghurt, if you like.

KEY LIME Tartlets

PREP TIME 25 MINUTES (+ STANDING & REFRIGERATION) MAKES 12

1½ cups (225g) raw cashews

⅔ cup (150g) fresh dates, pitted, chopped coarsely

1½ cups (115g) shredded coconut, toasted

2 tablespoons cacao powder

½ teaspoon sea salt flakes

⅔ cup (160g) cold-pressed extra-virgin coconut oil, melted

½ cup (125ml) lime juice

¼ cup (60ml) lemon juice

2 medium avocados (500g), chopped coarsely

⅓ cup (80ml) pure maple syrup

8 drops stevia

thinly sliced lime rind, to serve

1 Place cashews in a small bowl; cover with cold water. Stand, covered, for 2 hours. Drain cashews, then rinse under cold water; drain well.

2 Process one-third of the cashews until finely chopped. Add dates and process to form an almost smooth paste. Add shredded coconut, cacao, half the salt and 2 tablespoons of the coconut oil; pulse to combine.

3 Line a 12-hole (⅓-cup/80ml) muffin pan with 2 strips of baking paper in a cross, over base and up sides of holes. Press slightly heaped tablespoonfuls of the date mixture into each case, firmly pressing up against the sides. Refrigerate until needed.

4 Blend remaining cashews with remaining ingredients, using a high-powered blender, until mixture is a very smooth consistency. Spoon evenly among cases; refrigerate for at least 4 hours or until set. Serve topped with lime rind and micro herbs, if you like.

NUTRITIONAL COUNT PER TARTLET protein (5.1g); carbohydrate (18.5g); total fat (34.4g); fibre (4.9g)

MAKE & STASH Store tartlets in an airtight container in the fridge for up to 4 days.

Bliss Balls

PEANUT BUTTER & JELLY

PREP TIME 15 MINUTES
(+ REFRIGERATION)
MAKES 10

Combine 1 cup (120g) almond meal and ½ cup (40g) desiccated coconut in a medium bowl. Combine 2 tablespoons melted coconut oil, 2 tablespoons pure maple syrup, 1 teaspoon pure vanilla extract and ¼ cup (70g) crunchy peanut butter in a medium bowl; add to dry mixture and mix well. Roll tablespoonfuls of mixture into balls; place on a baking-paper-lined tray. Make small holes in the centres of balls with your finger; fill each hole with ¼ teaspoon of Raspberry Chia Jam (see page 219). Roll balls to enclose. Coat balls in your choice of topping (see page 209). Return balls to tray and refrigerate for 1 hour or until firm.

NUTRITIONAL COUNT PER BALL
protein (4.8g); carbohydrate (5.6g); total fat (16.5g); fibre (2.5g)

LORNA'S TIP Substitute Raspberry Chia Jam with fresh raspberries or dried cranberries. If using dried cranberries, you will need about 2 tablespoons.

SALTED CARAMEL WITH SPIRULINA

PREP TIME 20 MINUTES
(+ REFRIGERATION)
MAKES 12

Combine 1 cup (120g) almond meal, ½ cup (40g) desiccated coconut, 2 tablespoons cacao powder, 2 teaspoons spirulina and ¼ teaspoon pink himalayan salt in a medium bowl. Combine ¼ cup (70g) crunchy peanut butter, ¼ cup (60g) melted coconut oil, 2 tablespoons pure maple syrup and 1 teaspoon pure vanilla extract in a medium bowl. Add to dry mixture along with 5 pitted and finely chopped fresh dates (100g); mix well. Stand for 10 minutes to absorb liquid. Using wet hands, roll tablespoonfuls of mixture into balls; place on a baking-paper-lined tray. Coat balls in your choice of topping (see page 209); return to tray and refrigerate for 1 hour or until firm.

NUTRITIONAL COUNT PER BALL
protein (4.8g); carbohydrate (10.1g); total fat (15.9g); fibre (3.1g)

MAKE & STASH All bliss ball variations will keep in an airtight container in the fridge for up to 2 weeks.

LAMINGTON WITH CHIA JAM

PREP TIME 30 MINUTES
(+ REFRIGERATION)
MAKES 8

Combine 1 cup (120g) almond meal, ½ cup (40g) desiccated coconut, 2 tablespoons melted coconut oil, 2 tablespoons pure maple syrup and 1 teaspoon pure vanilla extract in a medium bowl; mix well. Roll tablespoonfuls of mixture into balls; place on a baking-paper-lined tray. Make small holes in the centres of balls with your finger; fill each hole with ¼ teaspoon of Raspberry Chia Jam (see page 219). Roll balls to enclose. Refrigerate for 30 minutes or until firm. Place 100g (3oz) chopped dark (70% cocoa) chocolate in a small heatproof bowl. Place bowl over a small saucepan of simmering water (don't let the base of the bowl touch the water); stir until melted. Dip balls in chocolate; coat in shredded coconut. Return to tray and refrigerate for 1 hour or until firm.

NUTRITIONAL COUNT PER BALL
protein (4.4g); carbohydrate (9.4g); total fat (21.4g); fibre (2.2g)

BLISS BALL *Toppings*

1

2

4

5

3

Each coating makes enough for 12 balls. Place your choice of coating on a plate. Using your hands, roll balls in coating; place balls on a baking-paper-lined tray and refrigerate for 1 hour or until firm.

FREEZE-DRIED BERRIES

½ cup (15g) freeze-dried raspberries or strawberries, crushed

BEE POLLEN

¼ cup (40g) bee pollen

SHREDDED COCONUT

⅔ cup (50g) shredded coconut

CACAO NIBS

⅓ cup (40g) cacao nibs, crushed

SESAME SEEDS

½ cup (80g) white sesame seeds, toasted lightly

PISTACHIOS

½ cup (70g) pistachios, chopped coarsely

LORNA'S TIP Coat bliss balls immediately after you shape them, when they are soft and moist; this makes it easier for the coating to stick.

MAKE & STASH Store bliss balls in an airtight container in the fridge for up to 2 weeks.

BLACKBERRY & YOGHURT *Sherbet*

PREP + COOK TIME 55 MINUTES (+ COOLING, REFRIGERATION & FREEZING) SERVES 4

3 cups (330g) chopped rhubarb

250g (8oz) fresh blackberries

½ cup (12g) stevia granules

1 teaspoon vanilla bean paste

1⅓ cups (375g) Greek-style yoghurt

½ cup (120g) labne (see Lorna's Tip)

½ cup (60g) frozen blackberries
   (optional)

WALNUT OAT CRUMBLE

⅔ cup (75g) coarsely chopped walnuts

½ cup (45g) rolled oats

¼ teaspoon mixed spice

30g (1oz) cold-pressed extra-virgin
   coconut oil, melted

1 free-range egg white, beaten lightly

1 Preheat oven to 200°C/400°F. Line two shallow-sided roasting pans or oven trays with baking paper.

2 Place rhubarb, fresh blackberries and stevia in one pan and toss to coat. Bake for 20 minutes or until fruit is soft. Cool.

3 Blend or process cooled rhubarb mixture, vanilla, yoghurt and labne until smooth. Cover and refrigerate until chilled.

4 Transfer rhubarb mixture to an ice-cream machine; churn following the manufacturer's instructions. Transfer to a shallow freezer-proof container; freeze for 3 hours or overnight until firm.

5 Meanwhile, to make walnut oat crumble, combine walnuts, oats, mixed spice and oil in a small bowl. Stir in egg white until oat mixture forms small clumps. Transfer mixture to second pan. Bake for 8 minutes or until light golden and crisp; cool.

6 Stand sherbet at room temperature for 10 minutes. Scoop sherbet into chilled glasses or bowls. Top with oat crumble and frozen blackberries; serve.

NUTRITIONAL COUNT PER SERVING protein (12.4g); carbohydrate (23.6g); total fat (33.1g); fibre (5.3g)

LORNA'S TIP Labne is a thick yoghurt cheese made from drained Greek yoghurt. It's available in some large supermarkets and from delis.

GINGER, COCONUT & *Almond Slice*

PREP TIME 35 MINUTES (+ STANDING & OVERNIGHT REFRIGERATION) MAKES 25

1½ cups (225g) raw cashews

1½ cups (240g) natural almonds

1 cup (140g) pitted dried dates,
chopped coarsely

½ cup (40g) shredded coconut

¾ cup (165g) crystallised ginger,
sliced thinly

¾ cup (180g) cold-pressed
extra-virgin coconut oil, melted

½ cup (125ml) pure maple syrup

1 young drinking coconut (1.2kg)

2 tablespoons finely grated ginger

½ cup (125ml) canned coconut milk

1½ teaspoons vanilla bean paste

1 Place cashews in a medium bowl; cover with cold water. Stand, covered, for 1 hour. Drain; rinse under cold water, then drain well.

2 Lightly oil a 23cm (9in) square cake pan with a little coconut oil; line base and sides with baking paper, extending the paper 5cm (2in) over the sides.

3 Process drained cashews and almonds until finely chopped. Add dates, shredded coconut, ¼ cup of the crystallised ginger, ¼ cup of the oil and 1 tablespoon of the maple syrup; pulse until combined. Press mixture into base of pan. Refrigerate until required.

4 Meanwhile, place coconut on its side on a board; carefully cut off the dome-shaped top with a cleaver or large knife – you will need to use a bit of force. Drain coconut water into a large jug (reserve coconut water for your next smoothie). Spoon out the soft coconut flesh; you should have about ½ cup (90g).

5 Blend or process fresh coconut flesh, fresh ginger, coconut milk, vanilla, remaining oil and maple syrup, and ¼ cup of the crystallised ginger until smooth. Pour mixture over biscuit base. Cover; refrigerate slice overnight.

6 Cut slice into 25 squares; serve topped with remaining crystallised ginger.

NUTRITIONAL COUNT PER PIECE protein (3.9g); carbohydrate (15.8g); total fat (19.8g); fibre (2.5g)

MAKE & STASH The slice will keep in an airtight container in the fridge for up to 1 week. It will freeze for up to 2 months; thaw in the fridge.

You will need to start this recipe a day ahead.

1

SUPER *lattes*

3

2

MINT MATCHA LATTE

PREP + COOK TIME 20 MINUTES SERVES 2

Stir 1 cup macadamia mylk and 1 cup coconut
mylk in a small saucepan over low-medium heat;
heat until just simmering. Remove from heat.
Add 8 peppermint tea bags; steep for 10 minutes.
Squeeze liquid from tea bags; discard bags. Pour
mylk into a medium bowl; whisk in 2 teaspoons
matcha green tea powder and 2 teaspoons pure
maple syrup. Serve warm or chilled, dusted with
a little extra matcha powder.

TURMERIC GINGER LATTE

PREP + COOK TIME 15 MINUTES SERVES 2

Stir 2 cups unsweetened almond mylk,
1 tablespoon pure maple syrup, 2 teaspoons
grated fresh turmeric, 1 cinnamon stick and
4 slices fresh ginger (10g) in a small saucepan
over low-medium heat; bring almost to boil.
Remove from heat; stand for 10 minutes. Strain
through a fine sieve into heatproof glasses; discard
solids. Serve dusted with ground cinnamon.

DELICIOUSLY PINK LATTE

PREP TIME 10 MINUTES SERVES 2

Push 2 large coarsely chopped beetroot (beets)
(400g) through a juice extractor into a jug.
You should have about ½ cup of juice. Place
beetroot juice in a medium bowl with 1½ cups
almond mylk; whisk to combine. Whisk in
1 teaspoon pure maple syrup (optional) and
½ teaspoon ground cinnamon. Serve chilled
or warmed.

MAKE & STASH All lattes can be stored in glass
jars in the fridge for up to 3 days. Stir just
before serving.

SECRET INGREDIENT
Frozen Passionfruit Cake

PREP + COOK TIME 55 MINUTES (+ REFRIGERATION, FREEZING & STANDING) SERVES 12

1½ cups (225g) natural seed mix

6 fresh dates (120g), pitted, chopped

1 tablespoon pure maple syrup

1 passionfruit

PASSIONFRUIT CURD

¾ cup (180ml) passionfruit pulp

½ cup (110g) pure maple sugar

185g (6oz) dairy-free spread

3 free-range eggs, plus 2 egg yolks

FILLING

2 cups (300g) raw cashews

300g (9½oz) cauliflower florets
   (see Lorna's Tip)

⅓ cup (80ml) passionfruit pulp

⅔ cup (160ml) pure maple syrup

2 teaspoons finely grated lemon rind

¼ cup (60ml) lemon juice

1 teaspoon pure vanilla extract

1 To make passionfruit curd, place ½ cup of the passionfruit pulp in a small food processor; pulse a few times to loosen the seeds from the pulp. Strain over a small bowl; discard seeds. Combine strained passionfruit, remaining passionfruit pulp, the sugar and spread in a small saucepan over medium heat until spread melts and sugar dissolves. Whisk eggs and egg yolks in a medium bowl until combined. Pour in passionfruit mixture, whisking constantly. Return mixture to pan over low heat; whisk constantly until mixture thickens and coats the back of a wooden spoon. Transfer mixture to a medium bowl; cover surface directly with plastic wrap. Cover; refrigerate for 2 hours or until set.

2 Grease an 18cm (7in) round springform pan; line base and side with baking paper.

3 Place seed mix, dates and maple syrup in a food processor; pulse until mixture just forms a sticky crumble and holds together when pressed. Press mixture firmly into base of pan. Freeze until required.

4 To make filling, place cashews in a medium bowl with enough cold water to cover. Stand for 30 minutes; drain. Steam cauliflower for 5 minutes or until tender; drain. Cool. Push passionfruit pulp through a sieve over a bowl; discard seeds. Blend cashews, cauliflower, passionfruit juice and remaining ingredients in a high-powered blender until smooth (be careful not to let the mixture overheat). Pour filling over frozen base in pan; smooth the surface. Freeze for 30 minutes.

5 Spoon chilled passionfruit curd over filling; smooth the surface. Cover; freeze overnight. Decorate frozen cake with passionfruit pulp before serving.

NUTRITIONAL COUNT PER SERVING protein (12.1g); carbohydrate (37.6g); total fat (35.1g); fibre (8.2g)

LORNA'S TIP You will need about 14 passionfruit for the curd, filling and decoration, and about ¼ medium (375g) cauliflower for the filling.

MAKE & STASH Frozen cake can be made up to 1 week ahead.

The filling uses cauliflower which gives a delicious, creamy taste. No one would ever guess that this cake doesn't have dairy in it.

VANILLA SPONGE WITH COCONUT YOGHURT
& Raspberry Chia Jam

PREP + COOK TIME 1 HOUR (+ STANDING & COOLING) SERVES 8

6 free-range eggs

2 teaspoons vanilla bean paste

¾ cup (165g) pure maple sugar

¼ cup (60g) cold-pressed
extra-virgin coconut oil, melted

1½ cups (180g) almond meal

¾ cup (120g) brown rice flour

1 teaspoon baking powder

500g (1lb) coconut yoghurt

125g (4oz) fresh raspberries

RASPBERRY CHIA JAM

1 cup (120g) frozen raspberries

1½ tablespoons pure maple syrup

2 teaspoons lemon juice

¼ teaspoon vanilla powder

1 tablespoon chia seeds

1 To make raspberry chia jam, blend raspberries, maple syrup, juice and vanilla powder until smooth. Transfer to a small saucepan; simmer for 3 minutes or until thickened. Stir in chia seeds. Pour into a jar and stand for 1 hour. (Makes 1 cup)

2 Preheat oven to 180°C/350°F. Grease two 20cm (8in) round cake pans; line bases with baking paper.

3 Beat eggs, vanilla paste and maple sugar in a bowl with an electric mixer for 10 minutes or until light and creamy. Add coconut oil; beat for a further 3 minutes. Gently stir in almond meal and combined sifted flour and baking powder. Divide mixture evenly between pans.

4 Bake cakes, rotating pans halfway through cooking, for 30 minutes or until cakes spring back when lightly touched in the centre. Turn cakes immediately, top-side down, onto wire racks to cool.

5 Place one cake layer on a serving plate; top with ¼ cup of the raspberry chia jam and half the yoghurt. Repeat layering with second cake, another ¼ cup jam and remaining yoghurt. (Reserve remaining jam for another use.) Top with fresh raspberries.

NUTRITIONAL COUNT PER SERVING protein (13.1g); carbohydrate (40.3g); total fat (36g); fibre (4.4g)

LORNA'S TIP Cake is best made on day of serving and assembled close to eating.

MAKE & STASH Keep jam refrigerated for up to 2 weeks, or freeze for up to 2 months.

CHOCOLATE *Fudge*

PREP + COOK TIME 30 MINUTES (+ REFRIGERATION) MAKES 30

2 cups (320g) blanched almonds

2 cups (160g) desiccated coconut

200g (6½oz) pitted medjool dates,
   chopped coarsely

½ cup (50g) cacao powder

2 teaspoons salt flakes

¼ cup (60ml) pure maple syrup

50g (1½oz) cocoa butter, melted

100 (3oz) dark chocolate (70% cocoa),
   chopped

2 teaspoons cold-pressed extra-virgin
   coconut oil

¼ cup (35g) macadamias, roasted,
   chopped coarsely

1 Grease and line a 20cm (8in) square cake pan with baking paper. Process almonds until finely ground. Add coconut and dates; process until mixture forms a soft paste. Add cacao, salt, maple syrup and cocoa butter; process until smooth. Press mixture into pan. Refrigerate for 2 hours or until firm.

2 Place chocolate and coconut oil in a small heatproof bowl over a small saucepan of simmering water (don't let the water touch the base of the bowl). Stir until chocolate mixture is melted and smooth.

3 Spread chocolate mixture over base in pan; sprinkle with macadamias. Refrigerate for 1 hour or until firm. Cut into 30 pieces.

NUTRITIONAL COUNT PER PIECE protein (3.5g); carbohydrate (8.4g); total fat (13.8g); fibre (2.9g)

MAKE & STASH Fudge can be made up to 1 week ahead.

SERVING SUGGESTIONS Fudge is delicious on its own, but it can also be served with a purchased dairy-free healthy ice-cream, or serve with my banana nice-cream on page 224.

COCONUT RED RICE *Pudding*

PREP + COOK TIME 50 MINUTES SERVES 4

¾ cup (150g) red rice, rinsed,
   drained (see Lorna's Tips)
2 cups (500ml) canned coconut milk
¼ cup (70g) pure maple sugar
¼ cup (60ml) canned coconut cream
   (see Lorna's Tips)
2 medium bananas (400g), sliced

1 Cook rice in a medium saucepan of boiling water for 30 minutes or until almost tender; drain.

2 Return rice to rinsed pan with coconut milk and sugar; bring to boil. Cook, stirring occasionally, for 15 minutes or until rice is tender and liquid thickens slightly.

3 Spoon rice into serving bowls; top with coconut cream and banana.

NUTRITIONAL COUNT PER SERVING protein (4.5g); carbohydrate (37.2g); total fat (23.3g); fibre (2.3g)

LORNA'S TIPS Red rice is available from large supermarkets, Asian grocery stores and some health food stores. I like to refrigerate the coconut cream in the carton or can for several hours and open the container without shaking it. It will give you some thick coconut cream on top; spoon the thick cream onto the pudding when serving along with some of the thinner cream underneath.

BANANA 'SPLIT' WITH ALMONDS
& Healthy Chocolate Sauce

PREP TIME 10 MINUTES SERVES 4

6 ripe medium bananas (1.2kg),
   cut into 1cm (½in) slices, frozen
½ cup (125ml) canned coconut milk
   or almond mylk (see Lorna's Tips)
4 small bananas (500g), extra
1 tablespoon chopped natural
   almonds
2 teaspoons cacao nibs
HEALTHY CHOCOLATE SAUCE
2 tablespoons cacao powder, sifted
¼ cup (60g) cold-pressed extra-virgin
   coconut oil, melted
2 tablespoons pure maple syrup

1 To make healthy chocolate sauce, combine all ingredients in a small bowl.

2 To make banana nice-cream, blend the frozen banana with coconut milk in a high-powered blender until smooth.

3 Peel extra bananas; split in half lengthways. Divide split bananas between bowls; top with scoops of banana nice-cream and drizzle with chocolate sauce. Sprinkle with almonds and cacao nibs; serve straight away.

NUTRITIONAL COUNT PER SERVING protein (5.5g); carbohydrate (53.2g); total fat (23g); fibre (5.7g)

LORNA'S TIPS Keep chopped bananas in a container in the freezer to make homemade nice-cream blending faster and easier. You can replace coconut milk with any mylk you prefer.

I want to show you that nutritious treats can be as good (if not better) than regular sugar-laden indulgences.

FLOURLESS CHOCOLATE CAKES WITH
Cacao & Matcha Lime Frostings

PREP + COOK TIME 45 MINUTES (+ COOLING) MAKES 12

3 free-range eggs, separated

⅔ cup (150g) pure maple sugar

1 teaspoon pure vanilla extract

75g (2½oz) dark chocolate
(70% cocoa), grated finely

¾ cup (75g) hazelnut meal

¼ cup (60g) cold-pressed
extra-virgin coconut oil, melted

CACAO FROSTING

1 large ripe avocado (320g)

2 tablespoons cacao powder

2 tablespoons cold-pressed
extra-virgin coconut oil, melted

2 tablespoons pure maple syrup

MATCHA LIME FROSTING

1 cup (240g) coconut yoghurt

1 tablespoon pure maple syrup

1 teaspoon matcha green tea powder

2 teaspoons finely grated lime rind

1 Preheat oven to 180°C/350°F. Line a 12-hole (⅓-cup/80ml) muffin pan with paper cases.

2 Beat egg yolks, ½ cup of the sugar and the vanilla with an electric mixer until thick and pale. Fold in combined chocolate and hazelnut meal.

3 Beat egg whites in a small bowl with an electric mixer until soft peaks form. Gradually add remaining sugar; beat until sugar dissolves between additions and mixture is glossy and stiff. Gently fold egg white mixture into egg yolk mixture with coconut oil. Pour into muffin pan.

4 Bake cakes for 20 minutes or until a skewer inserted into the centre of a cake comes out clean. Leave in pan for 10 minutes before transferring to a wire rack to cool completely.

5 To make cacao frosting, blend or process ingredients until smooth and glossy.

6 To make matcha lime frosting, combine all ingredients in a bowl until smooth.

7 Spread frostings onto six cakes each; dust with a little extra cacao and matcha powder, if you like.

NUTRITIONAL COUNT PER CAKE protein (4.4g); carbohydrate (20.5g); total fat (22.8g); fibre (1.3g)

MAKE & STASH Cakes can be made up to 3 days ahead; keep refrigerated in an airtight container. Stand at room temperature for 20 minutes before serving.

APPLE 'CRUMBLE' *Sundaes*

PREP + COOK TIME 40 MINUTES (+ COOLING) SERVES 6

1 cup (120g) pecans

1 tablespoon cold-pressed extra-virgin
coconut oil

4 large red apples (800g), unpeeled,
cored, cut into wedges

2 tablespoons pure maple syrup

1 tablespoon lemon juice

½ teaspoon finely grated ginger

½ teaspoon ground cinnamon

1 teaspoon arrowroot flour
(optional)

1 cup (240g) coconut yoghurt
(see Lorna's Tips)

MISO CARAMEL SAUCE

½ cup (125ml) pure maple syrup

¼ cup (70g) cashew spread (butter)
(see Lorna's Tips)

2 tablespoons white (shiro)
miso paste

½ teaspoon pure vanilla extract

1 To make miso caramel sauce, blend ingredients
until smooth.

2 Preheat oven to 170°C/340°F. Line an oven tray
with baking paper.

3 Place pecans on lined tray. Drizzle ¼ cup (60ml)
of the miso caramel sauce over pecans; toss to
coat evenly. Arrange in a single layer and bake for
15 minutes or until pecans are dark golden and
caramelised; cool. Place cooled pecans between two
sheets of baking paper; use a rolling pin to break into
large pieces of crumble.

4 Place coconut oil and apple in a large heavy-based
frying pan over low heat. Add maple syrup, juice,
ginger, cinnamon and arrowroot; stir to combine.
Cook, covered, stirring occasionally, for 10 minutes
or until apple is soft; uncover. Increase heat to medium;
cook for a further 5 minutes or until apple is dark
brown and almost caramelised. Cool.

5 Divide apple mixture among sundae glasses; top
each one with 2 tablespoons coconut yoghurt. Drizzle
with remaining miso caramel sauce and sprinkle with
pecan crumble; serve straight away.

NUTRITIONAL COUNT PER SERVING protein (6.5g);
carbohydrate (45.3g); total fat (30.6g); fibre (5.4g)

LORNA'S TIPS Use my coconut yoghurt recipe on
page 129 or a purchased yoghurt with no added
sugar. Cashew spread is available from major
supermarkets and health food stores.

RAW COOKIES & CREAM *Slice*

PREP TIME 35 MINUTES (+ STANDING & FREEZING) MAKES 30

¾ cup (115g) raw cashews
¾ cup (130g) activated buckwheat groats
¾ cup (120g) natural almonds
⅔ cup (50g) desiccated coconut
½ cup (50g) cacao powder
⅓ cup (80ml) pure maple syrup
¾ cup (180g) cold-pressed extra-virgin
   coconut oil, melted
½ teaspoon pure vanilla extract
2 young drinking coconuts (2.4kg)
1 cup (250ml) canned coconut cream
⅓ cup (80ml) pure maple syrup, extra
2 teaspoons pure vanilla extract, extra

1   Place cashews in a small bowl; cover with cold water. Stand, covered, for 4 hours or overnight. Drain cashews, then rinse under cold water; drain well.

2   Grease a 20cm (8in) square cake pan; line base and sides with baking paper, extending the paper 5cm (2in) over sides. Line an oven tray with baking paper.

3   Process buckwheat, almonds, desiccated coconut, cacao powder, maple syrup, ¼ cup of the coconut oil and the vanilla until mixture resembles coarse crumbs and just starts to come together; be careful not to over-process. Press two-thirds of mixture firmly into lined pan using a spatula. Press remaining mixture into a 1cm (½in) thick rectangle on lined tray. Freeze while preparing cream filling.

4   Place a coconut on its side on a chopping board. Carefully cut off the dome-shaped top with a cleaver or large knife; you will need to use a bit of force. Drain coconut water into a large jug (reserve coconut water for your next smoothie). Spoon out the soft flesh. Repeat with remaining coconut. Both coconuts should yield about 2 cups (180g) coconut flesh.

5   Blend coconut flesh, drained cashews, coconut cream, extra maple syrup and extra vanilla, using a high-powered blender, until very smooth. Add remaining coconut oil; blend until as smooth as possible. Pour over biscuit base in square pan.

6   Place biscuit rectangle from tray onto a cutting board; cut into 1cm (½in) pieces. Sprinkle pieces over cream filling, pressing in lightly. Freeze for 5 hours or until set.

7   Remove slice from pan 10 minutes before serving to soften slightly. Cut into 30 squares.

NUTRITIONAL COUNT PER PIECE protein (2.8g); carbohydrate (9.4g); total fat (14.9g); fibre (1.8g)

MAKE & STASH Store slice in an airtight container in the fridge for up to 5 days, or freeze for up to 2 months.

You will need to start this recipe a day ahead.

NATURAL REMEDIES & BEAUTY ELIXIRS

I believe that outer beauty is a direct reflection of your overall good health and that starts with what you eat – but is also dependant on how you manage your stress, whether you're getting regular exercise and, of course, drinking enough water. We need to take care of ourselves on the inside to look and feel good on the outside, but there are also some beauty remedies and elixirs that I use on a regular basis that I want to share with you, because I really do believe that when combined with a well-balanced diet and regular exercise, they work wonders to help combat the stresses of modern-day life. So whether you need some energy, you're fighting stress, want a little calm or are in need of a good detox – get ready to pamper yourself with totally natural and rejuvenating recipes that are my absolute favourites when I need a little self-care to get myself back on track.

INVIGORATE &
energise

Replenishing Energy Balm

1

Wake-up facial Mist

2

Peppermint foot scrub

REPLENISHING ENERGY BALM

PREP + COOK TIME 10 MINUTES (+ REFRIGERATION)
MAKES ½ CUP (125ML)

A replenishing balm infused with uplifting lemon grass that soothes muscles, reduces depression and energises your mood.

Heat ¼ cup apricot kernel oil, 2 tablespoons finely chopped cacao butter and 2 tablespoons yellow beeswax pastilles in a medium heatproof bowl over a small saucepan of boiling water (make sure the water doesn't touch the bowl). Remove from the heat and stir in 30 drops lemon grass essential oil. Working quickly so the balm doesn't set, stir in 2 teaspoons arrowroot or tapioca flour (starch) until combined. Pour balm into a clean 125ml glass jar or container. Refrigerate for 15 minutes or until set. Apply liberally to your arms, legs, torso, feet and hands; massage into skin until absorbed. Suitable for dry and sensitive skin. Store in a cool place away from direct sunlight. Keeps for 3 months.

WAKE-UP FACIAL MIST

PREP TIME 2 MINUTES MAKES 100ML

Packed full of probiotics, this refreshing facial mist cools, soothes and softens the skin while the scent is invigorating.

Combine ¼ cup kombucha and 2 tablespoons orange blossom water in a clean 100ml spray bottle; shake well. Spray over face and neck; allow to air dry. Suitable for sensitive and oily skin types. Store in the fridge and shake well before use. Keeps for 3 months.

PEPPERMINT FOOT SCRUB

PREP TIME 5 MINUTES MAKES 1½ CUPS (375ML)

Smooth and soften your feet with this invigorating and refreshing peppermint foot scrub that will be sure to put a bounce in your step.

Combine 1 cup fine sea salt, ½ cup bicarbonate of soda (baking soda) and 1 teaspoon spirulina in a medium bowl. Add ¼ cup melted coconut oil, 2 tablespoons honey and 20 drops peppermint essential oil; mix well. Transfer mixture to a clean 375ml glass jar or container. Massage mixture in a slow circular motion over dry feet, focusing on the dry skin around the heels and balls of the feet; wash off with warm water. Suitable for dry and normal skin types. Store in a cool, dry place away from direct sunlight. Keeps for 1 month.

LORNA'S TIP Soak your feet in warm water for 10 minutes to soften the skin before using the scrub.

Restore

2

1

RESTORATIVE HAIR MASK

PREP TIME 5 MINUTES MAKES ½ CUP (125ML) OR 1 MASK

An antioxidant-rich mask infused with essential oils that hydrates, restores and strengthens damaged hair and soothes an irritated scalp.

Blend 1 medium ripe avocado and 1 tablespoon each of honey and extra-virgin olive oil until smooth. Add 10 drops lavender and 8 drops rosemary essential oils; blend to combine. Apply to damp hair, starting at the ends. Work into the scalp; comb through hair. Twist hair and cover with a shower cap. Leave in for 40 minutes, then rinse thoroughly. Shampoo and condition your hair as normal. Suitable for damaged and dry hair. Mask is best used straight away. Leftovers can be stored in an airtight container in the fridge for up to 3 days.

BEET & ROSE LIP SALVE

PREP + COOK TIME 10 MINUTES (+ REFRIGERATION)
MAKES ¹/₃ CUP (80ML)

Soothe and repair dry and cracked lips with this hydrating lip balm.

Melt ¼ cup coconut oil, 1 tablespoon yellow beeswax pastilles and 1 teaspoon vitamin E oil in a medium heatproof bowl over a small saucepan of boiling water (make sure the water doesn't touch the bowl). Remove from heat. Whisk in 40 drops rose essential oil and 2 teaspoons fresh beetroot juice; whisk vigorously until the mixture emulsifies. Spoon into small containers and refrigerate for 15 minutes or until set. Apply liberally to your lips whenever they feel dry. Suitable for all skin types. Store in a cool, dry place away from direct sunlight. Keeps for 1 month.

LORNA'S TIPS Balm can also be used as a multipurpose moisturiser on your cuticles, elbows and heels. Pure rose essential oil is very hard to find (and expensive); most are diluted to varying strengths so adjust as needed.

MAGNESIUM BODY SCRUB

PREP TIME 5 MINUTES MAKES 1½ CUPS (375ML)

A rejuvenating scrub made with magnesium salts that helps skin hydration, improves circulation, relaxes muscles and relieves pain.

Blend 1½ cups magnesium salt flakes until they resemble the consistency of fine sea salt; transfer to a medium mixing bowl. Add ¼ cup dried lavender flowers, ¼ cup almond oil and 35 drops lavender essential oil; mix well. Massage scrub onto your skin in circular motions until it crumbles away, avoiding your face and neck. Wash off with warm water. Suitable for dry skin. Store in an airtight container in a cool, dry place away from direct sunlight. Keeps for 1 month.

SKIN
Glow

1

Intense
Hydrating
Hair Serum

2

Calming
face Mask

INTENSE HYDRATING HAIR SERUM

PREP TIME 5 MINUTES MAKES 50ML

This serum is infused with essential oils that promote hair growth, strengthen hair and soothe scalp irritations, leaving your hair soft and silky.

Combine 1 tablespoon each of argan oil and castor oil and 2 teaspoons vitamin E oil in a 100ml glass bottle with a pump or eyedropper. Add 40 drops chamomile and 10 drops rosemary essential oils; shake well. To use, rub a few drops of serum between your palms; rub into the ends and mid-section of dry hair. Massage excess oil into scalp. Leave in for 20 minutes (or overnight); shampoo and condition hair as normal. You can also apply serum to ends of towel-dried hair; comb through. Suitable for dry and damaged hair. Store in a cool, dry place away from direct sunlight. Keeps for 6 months.

LORNA'S TIP If leaving in overnight, place a clean old towel over your pillow.

CALMING FACE MASK

PREP TIME 5 MINUTES MAKES ¹/₃ CUP (80ML) OR 1–2 MASKS

Packed full of antioxidants, this moisturising face mask soothes and softens skin, leaving it with a healthy and youthful glow.

Blend ½ medium ripe avocado, 1 tablespoon cacao powder and 1 tablespoon honey in a small blender until smooth. Stir in 2 drops peppermint essential oil. Apply mask to face and neck, avoiding eye area. Leave on for 10–15 minutes, then wash off with warm water. Suitable for all skin types. Mask is best used straight away, but leftovers can be stored in an airtight container in the fridge for up to 3 days.

3

CARROT SEED EYE CREAM

PREP TIME 10 MINUTES (+ REFRIGERATION) MAKES ¹/₃ CUP (80ML)

Carrot seed oil is one of the best essential oils for treating dry and aging skin. This cream reduces puffiness, dark circles and smoothes fine lines.

Melt ¼ cup chopped cacao butter, 1 tablespoon almond oil, ¼ teaspoon each evening primrose and rosehip essential oils in a medium heatproof bowl over a small saucepan of boiling water (make sure the water doesn't touch the bowl). Remove from the heat; stir in 5 drops carrot seed essential oil. Refrigerate for 15 minutes or until partially solidified (you should be able to make a dent in the cream). Whisk until it resembles a creamed-butter consistency. Transfer to clean glass jar or container and refrigerate for 15 minutes or until set. To use, dab a tiny amount under the eye along the eye socket with your ring finger. Be careful not to apply the cream too close to your eyes. Store in a cool place away from direct sunlight. Keeps for 3 months.

Detox

NATURAL TEETH WHITENER

PREP TIME 1 MINUTE MAKES 1 TREATMENT

Polishes and whitens teeth, leaving them feeling smooth and clean.

Place 1 teaspoon activated coconut charcoal in a small bowl. Wet a toothbrush; shake off excess water and pat dry. Dip a toothbrush into charcoal; brush teeth in small circles for 2–3 minutes, then thoroughly rinse your mouth several times. Brush your teeth (and tongue) with a different toothbrush and toothpaste.

LORNA'S TIPS Charcoal is known for its ability to absorb toxins. It's potent and should not be used daily. It is also very messy – your mouth will turn black. The powder stains skin, tiles and clothing, so keep a damp sponge on hand. You can buy it from health food stores; if unavailable, use bicarbonate of soda (baking soda) mixed with a few drops of lemon juice.

BENTONITE CLAY FACE MASK

PREP TIME 5 MINUTES MAKES 2 TABLESPOONS OR 3 FACE MASKS

This antioxidant-packed clay mask draws toxins from your skin, helps prevent breakouts and reduces skin inflammation and redness.

Mix 1 tablespoon each bentonite clay powder, lime juice and filtered water in a small glass bowl to a paste. Stir in 2 teaspoons matcha green tea powder and 4 drops lime essential oil. Apply mask to face and neck, avoiding eye area. Leave on for 10 minutes; wash off with warm water. Suitable for oily and acne-prone skin. Mask is best used straight away, but leftovers can be stored in an airtight container in the fridge for up to 1 week.

LORNA'S TIP Bentonite clay is rich in nutrients and minerals and is known for its detoxifying properties. When mixing, use non-metallic bowls and spoons, as it is said the clay can absorb some of the properties of the metal.

COCONUT LIME CLAY BODY SCRUB

PREP TIME 5 MINUTES MAKES 1 CUP (250ML)

The French clay absorbs impurities while the sugar and coconut polish away dead skin, leaving your skin feeling dewy and soft.

Combine ½ cup raw caster sugar, ½ cup shredded coconut and ¼ cup white French clay in a medium bowl. Add 2 tablespoons grated lime rind and 2 tablespoons coconut yoghurt; mix to a paste. Stir in 10 drops lime essential oil. Standing in a dry bath or shower recess, coat arms, legs and torso with the paste, massaging in slow circular motions. Leave clay scrub on for 15 minutes before rinsing. Suitable for all skin types. Store leftovers in an airtight container in the fridge for up to 1 week.

FIGHTING Stress

1 — pulse-point Aromatherapy oil.

2 — de Stress body lotion

deep Sleep
Pillow Spray

PULSE POINT AROMATHERAPY OIL

PREP TIME 2 MINUTES MAKES 25ML

Infused with chamomile and lavender to help to relieve tension, settle nerves and calm the mind and body – promoting a better night's sleep.

Combine 1 tablespoon almond oil, 35 drops chamomile and 15 drops lavender essential oils in a 25ml glass bottle with a roll-cap or eyedropper; shake well. Massage a few drops onto pulse points – the temples, behind ears and inside of wrists. Use on one point at a time. Suitable for all skin types. Store in a cool, dry place away from direct sunlight. Keeps for 6 months.

LORNA'S TIP Keep this oil in your bedside drawer – it's great for insomnia, especially when paired with the Deep Sleep Pillow Spray (see below).

DE-STRESS BODY LOTION

PREP + COOK TIME 25 MINUTES (+ FREEZING) MAKES 400ML

A velvety soft lotion infused with the sweet scent of orange and jasmine – it doubles as a calming night cream and helps to relax the mind and body.

Melt ⅓ cup each of shea butter, sunflower oil and almond oil in a medium heatproof bowl over a small saucepan of boiling water (make sure the water doesn't touch the bowl). Remove from heat; stir in 60 drops orange and 30 drops jasmine essential oils. Freeze for 1 hour until partially solidified (you should be able to make a dent in it). Beat in a small bowl with an electric mixer until smooth and mixture reaches room temperature (it is important the oil is the same temperature as the water when you combine them). Check lotion for aroma and adjust. Very slowly add 1 cup distilled water in a thin stream, beating continuously until a mayonnaise consistency. Continue beating for 5 minutes, then pour into clean glass jars or bottles with lotion pumps. Massage over body, feet and hands. Suitable for dry skin. As this lotion contains water, it has a shorter shelf life. Store in a cool place away from direct sunlight. Keeps for 1 week, or 1 month if kept in the fridge.

DEEP SLEEP PILLOW SPRAY

PREP TIME 2 MINUTES MAKES 100ML

Infused with lavender and rose to soothe an over-stimulated mind and help with relaxation and sleep.

Combine 100ml rose water (or distilled water) with 25 drops lavender essential oil in a 100ml spray bottle. Shake well before use. Spray a fine mist over your pillow just before bed. You can also spray a small amount around the room. Suitable for all skin types. Store in a cool, dry place away from direct sunlight. Keeps for 3 months.

Glossary

BARLEY a nutritious grain used in soups and stews. Hulled barley, the least processed, is high in fibre. Pearl barley has had the husk removed, then been steamed and polished so that only the 'pearl' remains, much the same as white rice.

BUCKWHEAT a herb in the same plant family as rhubarb; not a cereal so it is gluten free. Available as flour: ground (cracked) into coarse, medium or fine granules (kasha) and used similarly to polenta; or as groats: the whole kernel sold roasted as a cereal product.

CACAO POWDER raw cacao powder is made by removing the cocoa butter using a process known as cold-pressing. It retains more of its nutrients than heat-processed cocoa powder; it also has a stronger, more bitter chocolate taste.

CHIA SEEDS contain protein and all the essential amino acids, as well as being fibre rich and a wealth of vitamins, minerals and antioxidants.

CHICKPEAS (GARBANZO BEANS) an irregularly round, sandy-coloured legume.

DAIKON also called white radish. Peel and eat raw in salads or use shredded.

DUKKAH an Egyptian specialty spice mixture made up of roasted nuts, seeds and an array of aromatic spices.

EDAMAME are shelled soybeans that are usually bought frozen. They are available from Asian food stores and major supermarkets.

HARISSA a North African paste made from dried red chillies, garlic, olive oil and caraway seeds; can be used as a rub for meat, an ingredient in sauces and dressings, or served as a condiment. It is available from Middle Eastern food shops and some supermarkets.

MAPLE SYRUP, PURE distilled from the sap of sugar maple trees found only in Canada and the USA. Maple-flavoured or pancake syrup is not an adequate substitute.

MISO fermented soybean paste. There are many types of miso, each with their own aroma, flavour, colour and texture. Miso can be kept, airtight, for up to a year in the fridge.

OIL
coconut is extracted from the coconut flesh to produce an oil that is generally solid at room temperature. Usually, you need to heat it to use, unless otherwise stated in the recipe. The best quality is virgin coconut oil, which is the oil pressed from the dried coconut flesh and doesn't include the use of solvents or other refining processes.
olive made from ripened olives. Extra virgin and virgin are the first and second press of the olives; 'light' refers to taste not fat levels.

PEPITAS (PUMPKIN SEED KERNELS) the green kernels (seeds) of dried pumpkin seeds; available plain or salted.

QUINOA pronouced keen-wa. A seed not a grain with a delicate, slightly nutty taste and chewy texture. Quinoa is gluten free.

STERILISING JARS it's important the jars be as clean as possible; make sure your hands, the preparation area, tea towels and cloths etc are clean too. The aim is to finish sterilising the jars and lids at the same time the mixture is ready to be bottled; the mixture should be bottled into hot, dry, clean jars. Jars that aren't sterilised properly can cause deterioration of the contents during storage. Always start with cleaned washed jars and lids, then follow one of these methods:

(1) Put the jars and lids through the hottest cycle of a dishwasher without using any detergent.

(2) Lie the jars down in a boiler with the lids, cover with cold water, then cover with a lid. Bring to boil over high heat and boil the jars for 20 minutes.

(3) Stand the jars upright, without touching each other, on a wooden board on the lowest oven shelf. Turn oven onto the lowest possible temperature; leave jars to heat for 30 minutes.

Remove jars from the oven or dishwasher with a towel, or from the boiling water with tongs and rubber-gloved hands; the water will evaporate from hot wet jars quite quickly. Stand jars upright, and not touching each other, on a wooden board or a bench covered with a towel. Fill jars as directed in the recipe; secure the lids tightly, holding jars firmly with a towel or an oven mitt. Leave filled jars at room temperature to cool before storing.

STEVIA comes from the leaves of a plant so is promoted as a natural sweetener. It is processed into a white powder that can be used in a similar way to sugar. It has a minimal effect on blood glucose levels and has no kilojoules so can be a useful way to reduce your sugar intake.

SUMAC a purple-red, astringent spice ground from berries growing on shrubs that flourish wild around the Mediterranean; adds a tart, lemony flavour to dips and dressings and goes well with barbecued meat, particularly lamb. Can be found in Middle Eastern food stores.

TAHINI a rich, sesame-seed paste; available from supermarkets and health food stores.

TAMARI a thick, dark soy sauce made mainly from soybeans but without the wheat used in most standard soy sauces.

TOFU also called bean curd; an off-white, custard-like product made from the 'milk' of crushed soybeans. Comes fresh as soft or firm, and processed as fried or pressed dried sheets.

Conversion Chart

MEASURES

One Australian metric measuring cup holds approximately 250ml; one Australian metric tablespoon holds 20ml; one Australian metric teaspoon holds 5ml.

The difference between one country's measuring cups and another's is within a two- or three-teaspoon variance and will not affect your cooking results. North America, New Zealand and the United Kingdom use a 15ml tablespoon.

All cup and spoon measurements are level. The most accurate way of measuring dry ingredients is to weigh them. When measuring liquids, use a clear glass or plastic jug with the metric markings.

The imperial measurements used in these recipes are approximate only. Measurements for cake pans are approximate only. Using same-shaped cake pans of a similar size should not affect the outcome of your baking. We measure the inside top of the cake pan to determine sizes.

We use large eggs with an average weight of 60g.

DRY MEASURES

METRIC	IMPERIAL
15G	½OZ
30G	1OZ
60G	2OZ
90G	3OZ
125G	4OZ (¼LB)
155G	5OZ
185G	6OZ
220G	7OZ
250G	8OZ (½LB)
280G	9OZ
315G	10OZ
345G	11OZ
375G	12OZ (¾LB)
410G	13OZ
440G	14OZ
470G	15OZ
500G	16OZ (1LB)
750G	24OZ (1½LB)
1KG	32OZ (2LB)

LIQUID MEASURES

METRIC	IMPERIAL
30ML	1 FLUID OZ
60ML	2 FLUID OZ
100ML	3 FLUID OZ
125ML	4 FLUID OZ
150ML	5 FLUID OZ
190ML	6 FLUID OZ
250ML	8 FLUID OZ
300ML	10 FLUID OZ
500ML	16 FLUID OZ
600ML	20 FLUID OZ
1000ML (1 LITRE)	1¾ PINTS

LENGTH MEASURES

METRIC	IMPERIAL
3MM	⅛IN
6MM	¼IN
1CM	½IN
2CM	¾IN
2.5CM	1IN
5CM	2IN
6CM	2½IN
8CM	3IN
10CM	4IN
13CM	5IN
15CM	6IN
18CM	7IN
20CM	8IN
22CM	9IN
25CM	10IN
28CM	11IN
30CM	12IN (1FT)

OVEN TEMPERATURES

The oven temperatures in this book are for conventional ovens; if you have a fan-forced oven, decrease the temperature by 10–20 degrees.

	°C (CELSIUS)	°F (FAHRENHEIT)
VERY SLOW	120	250
SLOW	150	300
MODERATELY SLOW	160	325
MODERATE	180	350
MODERATELY HOT	200	400
HOT	220	425
VERY HOT	240	475

Index